Power, innovation, and problem-solving in personnel management

Karen Legge

MRC Social and Applied Psychology Unit,
Department of Psychology,
The University, Sheffield

McGRAW-HILL Book Company (UK) Limited

London · New York · St Louis · San Francisco · Auckland
Bogotá · Guatemala · Hamburg · Johannesburg · Lisbon
Madrid · Mexico · Montreal · New Delhi · Panama · Paris
San Juan · São Paulo · Singapore · Sydney · Tokyo · Toronto

Published by:
McGRAW-HILL Book Company (UK) Limited
MAIDENHEAD ● BERKSHIRE ● ENGLAND

British Library Cataloguing in Publication Data
Legge, Karen
Power, innovation, and problem-solving in personnel management
  1. Personnel management
  I. Title
  658.3   HF5549   77-30333
ISBN 0-07-084078-4

234 JWA   8543

Printed and bound in Great Britain

To Enid, Tom, and Dan

Contents

Preface

Many books now exist which deal with personnel management, so why another? The answer lies in the direction this book takes which differs from that of many of the standard student texts in this area. Rather than offering generalized prescriptions as do the majority of texts, it seeks to show why, in practice, such prescriptions may prove at worst irrelevant and at best of disappointing applicability to the student once he has left the classroom for the real world of practical management. For, it is argued, not only does much of the reputed 'best practice' rest on 'special case' models and, hence, may be inappropriate to those organizational circumstances that do not directly correspond to them, but 'best practice' tends to ignore the constraints arising from the political realities of organizational behaviour that circumscribe any manager's freedom and ability to pursue a given course of action. In contrast, employing an analysis of the actual behaviour of managers, exercising this function in a range of organizations and environments, this book seeks to alert students to the reality that not only may personnel managers' traditional lack of power and influence in this area hinder the establishment of even such recognized 'best practice' as would suit their organizational circumstances and requirements, but that this lack of authority may be further exacerbated by attempts to implement irrelevant or inappropriate 'best practice'. These issues raise two major and inter-related themes of this book. First, is there, and if so, why is there, a genuine lack of authority in the roles of personnel specialists (or of other managers when they attempt to tackle 'personnel' problems)? If so, what innovative strategies may be adopted to augment this authority? Second, to what extent can contingency theory be used to tackle the design of an authoritative, viable personnel function and development of effective personnel practice in different organizational contexts?

Generally speaking, it is to these questions, and the critique and analysis on which they rest, rather than to the advocacy of general prescriptions on substantive matters, that the subsequent chapters are devoted; hopefully to provide a corrective, but companion volume to the standard tests.

More specifically, the arguments of the book are developed as follows:

Chapter 1 suggests that while students of personnel management (and practising personnel managers for that matter) seek the answer to two basic questions from the standard textbooks, namely 'What should be the objectives of personnel management?' and 'How do I set about achieving them?', the answers provided are of limited practical help. This is for three main reasons. The textbooks fail to recognize that the underpinnings of their normative approach are problematic; nevertheless, they tend to make general prescriptions on the basis of this shaky foundation, prescriptions which consistently neglect adequate consideration of the influence of contextual factors on policy design and implementation, and finally they assume without question that personnel managers at the operating level have sufficient power to implement their prescriptions—whether relevant to their organization's requirements or not. Unfortunately, these in-adequacies can generate mutually reinforcing ill effects. For personnel management students who later base their policy and practice on such textbook prescriptions are likely to contribute to and maintain the lack of status and influence that their function traditionally has commanded, as their activities, often irrelevant or inappropriate to their organization's particular needs, tend to lack credibility.

This introduces the main theme of the book: that without power and influence in organizational decision-making, a personnel manager cannot hope to successfully implement *any* sophisticated personnel strategy—let alone that advocated by the textbooks. Consequently, questions about how the personnel function can gain or increase its power must be considered in conjunction with the substantive questions about what constitutes 'good' personnel management in specified organizational contexts.

Thus, **chapters 2, 3 and 4** consider the relationship between the personnel function and organizational power. **Chapter 2** focuses on two preliminary definitional questions, 'what exactly *is* the personnel function about which the textbooks talk so glibly?' and 'what are the sources of power available for its managers to exploit, both as representatives of and individual competitors within the function?' The influence of ambiguities and confusions about the purpose, scope, and boundaries of the function on its ability to gain recognition are examined, along with the range of inter-related factors that, it is suggested, determines a personnel manager's power to implement the policies he believes to be appropriate. **Chapter 3** goes on to examine the truth of the traditional stereotype of the personnel function as lacking in power and status in the majority of organizations—at least up until the early to mid 1970s. Evidence is presented to illustrate, in a variety of British and American organizational contexts, that both the human resource dimension to industrial problems and the personnel specialists who should have been advocating this perspective, have been neglected in organizational decision-making, with deleterious results. In addition, arguments are advanced to suggest why, and in what circumstances, this has occurred.

Having considered some of the organizational problems stemming from inadequate or ineffectual personnel management in case-study examples in chapter 3, the question then posed in **chapters 4, 5 and 6** is 'how can this state of affairs be rectified?' The answer would seem to lie in three subsidiary questions: 'how can the personnel function gain sufficient power to become an influential voice in organizational decision-making?', 'what should be its approach to personnel policy and practice, both to gain and maintain capability and support and to contribute to organizational effectiveness (however defined)?'; and 'how should a specialist personnel department be designed to facilitate the achievement of these objectives?'

In **chapter 4** the answer to the first of these questions, concerning the acquisition of power, is seen to lie partly in continuing organizational and environmental changes (e.g., political and legislative developments, increased militancy on the part of blue collar workers, the organization of white collar, technical, and managerial staff), and partly in the personnel specialists' own search for professional authority. Professional authority for the personnel specialist can derive from any of three paths, depending on organizational circumstances. These comprise conformist innovation (when the personnel manager acquires expertise that enables him to demonstrate a closer relationship between his activities and organizational success criteria), deviant innovation (when the personnel manager uses his professional competence to gain acceptance for a different set of criteria for the evaluation of organizational success and his contribution to it), and through a role that can encompass both approaches, that of the problem-solver.

It is in the role of the problem-solver, whether orientated towards conformist or deviant innovation solutions, that an answer to the second question, about the personnel manager's approach to evolving effective policy and practice, may perhaps best be found. **Chapter 5** argues that diagnostic problem-solving demands a contingent approach, in other words the design and implementation of policy that matches, or is *contingent* upon specified organizational requirements and circumstances. The five main steps involved in carrying out this approach are analysed and illustrated with reference to three major personnel activities (the design and management of wage payment systems, the design and implementation of job design exercises, and the development of managerial styles appropriate to different categories of decision-making).

Finally, **chapter 6** tackles the third question about the design of a specialist personnel department to facilitate the achievement of more effective personnel management. It is argued that a contingent approach should direct this design exercise also, so that the structure and nature of the roles in the personnel department match the organizational context in which the department is to operate. The steps involved, including how to model organizational context, both structurally and processually and how to relate the resulting models of context to a matrix of specialist personnel roles and relationships, are described and illustrated by examples.

The book concludes with a summary of the main themes explored and the conclusions tentatively reached.

Acknowledgements

To the MRC Social and Applied Psychology Unit, Sheffield, which allowed me time to write, to colleagues and friends both at Sheffield and Manchester Business School who both encouraged me and suffered with me in the writing, and to Carol Jones, Flavia Shrivastava, and Valerie Wood, who suffered for me in typing the manuscript, my grateful thanks are extended.

Karen Legge
May 1977

1. The problem stated

Two fundamental questions confront any student or practising manager who becomes involved in the personnel function:

What should be the objectives of personnel management?
How do I achieve them?

It is to these two fundamental questions that most of the literature on personnel management addresses itself. Yet, because it tends to treat these questions as non-problematic and amenable to a straightforward set of replies, not only has it become stylized in approach, but ultimately it begs the questions that it pretends to answer. The root of the problem is reflected in three traits that characterize most 'personnel texts' (e.g., Pigors and Myers, 1969; Megginson, 1972; Miner and Miner, 1973; Glueck, 1974; Lyons, 1971; Cuming, 1975).

1. They tend to be normative rather than positive.
2. They tend to be prescriptive in general terms rather than analytical about actual situations.
3. They tend to discuss the content of the function removed from its context without recognizing that, in practice, it is the context in which it operates that is likely to constrain and mould the content of the function.

Each of these characteristics is logically related to the others and hence the literature presents a high, and superficially persuasive, level of logical consistency. However, this apparent integrity has ultimately proved dysfunctional, as it has perpetuated a style of writing that is unable to satis-

1

factorily answer the two fundamental questions that it sets out to tackle. What are the grounds for this charge?

Personnel texts: their normative approach. 'What should be the objectives of personnel management?' Most personnel texts, written with practitioners or would be practitioners in mind,[1] take this question as a starting point for discussions that are more vocational than academic in intent, concerned, as Glueck puts it with 'people in the workplace—what can and is and should be done for them' (1974, page 1). Although the emphasis is clearly on practice, in spite of Glueck's mention of what *is* and *can* be done, most writers tend to concentrate on what *should* be undertaken as part of personnel management and to ignore what has actually been observed to be done, warts and all, by managers in this area.[2] In other words, the approach tends to be normative (what should be done) rather than positive (what in fact is observed to be done) in orientation. This is to be expected: potential practitioners want to know first and foremost what they should be doing irrespective of their knowledge of actual personnel management practices they have experienced—or, perhaps, because of their lack of it! If experienced practitioners, they want to measure up their own personnel practices with the so-called 'best practice' to be found within the covers of an up-to-date text. However, before the authors of these texts can prescribe any course of action for the practitioners, they recognize that, in order to give it direction, confident prescription needs to rest on some value position.

Thus, Miner and Miner make reference to their 'provision of a value system in terms of which the techniques and procedures of personnel management may be appraised' (1973, page v). The normative stance they take is similar to that adopted by most prescriptive writers on personnel management. In other words 'reference to the fact that a personnel manager *should* do this or that means that by doing so he will in all probability contribute most effectively to the goals of the organization and thus to the fulfilment of his managerial responsibilities' (1973, page v). This may be compared with Megginson's comment that the manager's function must be 'to combine physical resources, human resources, and

---

[1] See, for example, Megginson (1972, page ix) 'it is hoped that the managers of the future will find some enlightenment from this material which will help them to resolve their personnel problems more rationally and analytically'; Glueck (1974, page 1) 'For whom is the book written? For all those interested in or responsible for people in the workplace: supervisors, managers, administrators (or would-be supervisors, managers, and administrators), and those directly responsible for the people function in a work organization, whether they call themselves personnel, manpower or employee-relation specialists'; Strauss and Sayles (1960, page vi) 'This book is addressed to the student of business who wants to equip himself to deal effectively with the human problems of the business organization'.

[2] An exception here is McFarland (1968), who incorporates into his textbook, often as cautionary tales, some of the findings of his earlier study *Company Officers Assess the Personnel Function* (AMA Research Report No. 79, New York: American Management Association, 1967) on what personnel managers were actually perceived to be and to do in a range of US companies.

technology into a productive system that will foster the attainment of individual enterprise, and national objectives' (1972, page 20); or with Glueck's that 'the goals of the personnel department necessarily involve the goals of the whole organization' (1974, page 13); or with that of Towle *et al.*, that 'successful personnel management implies that these functions and activities (the acquisition, development, and maintenance of human resources) integrate the efforts of people with the other resources of an organization in such a manner that the objectives of the company, the goals of individual workers, and the goals of society at large are all attained in the highest degree compatible with the work situation' (1972, page 5).

However, although most writers on personnel management either implicitly or explicitly accept that good personnel management should aim for 'the optimum utilization of human resources in order to achieve the goals and objectives of the organization', this apparently unequivocal value position blurs on further examination.

One problem is that easy reference to individual, organizational, and societal goals ignores the confusion that has surrounded the use of the goal concept, especially in relation to organizations.[3] Many writers would argue that, at an operational level, organizational goals are often hard to pin down, that, strictly speaking, organizations (or societies, for that matter) do not have goals, only individuals do, and that this being so, the utility of the concept is questionable as it implies a degree of consensus between individual decision-makers that is unlikely to exist (Cyert and March, 1963; Simon, 1967; Perrow, 1961, 1970a). Instead, they suggest that 'coalitions' of managers seek to achieve multiple objectives simultaneously or in sequence, which may change over time, and which may or may not be consistent with those objectives which other 'coalitions' within the organization are, at the same time, pursuing.

Much of this confusion seems to have arisen over a frequent failure, only too evident in many personnel management texts, to differentiate between goals which may be ends in themselves (e.g., maximization of profit, the optimum standard of patient care, the pursuit of academic excellence in teaching and research), and about which there is likely to be a reasonable level of consensus within the organization, and goals which are means to these ends, and about which there is likely to be considerable debate and conflict.[4] (This distinction is similar to that made by Perrow, between

[3] For a short summary of the different, and sometimes incompatible, ways this concept has been used, see Bowey, A. M., *The Sociology of Organisations*, London: Hodder and Stoughton, 1976, pages 59–64.

[4] Of course, in practice, it may be difficult to distinguish between a goal that exists as an end in itself and one that is a means to that end. As Perrow (1970a, page 134) writes, 'What one observer calls a goal, another may equally well designate as a means towards some higher or more general goal. Profit, for example, may be viewed as a goal, or as a means of rewarding stockholders or ensuring growth (the "real" goals).' Perrow himself attempts to overcome this problem of differentiation by distinguishing five types or levels of goals—societal, output, system, product and derived goals—a classification resting on a system perspective of organization.

'official' goals—statements of intent for organizations as a whole—and 'operative goals'—the ends sought through the actual operating policies of the organization, which are tied more directly to group interests and may either support, be irrelevant to, or even subvert official goals.) Indeed, such disputes as do exist about the ends an organization might pursue, are more usually provoked by doubts as to feasibility (i.e., uncertainty about the *means* of achievement) rather than by disagreement about the *end* in itself.

In practice, the personnel function in particular tends to become enmeshed in this confusion, as not only is it often difficult to show a clear-cut relationship between the tasks it undertakes and those organizational goals whose achievement is expressed in financial terms, but often its brief is to work for the achievement of goals reflecting such intangibles as organizational ethos, which is difficult to define and a problem to measure. An example of the latter is illustrated in the objectives sought by OD programmes, which have been described as 'those optimizing human and social improvement or as those optimizing task accomplishment or more likely as some (often confused) blend of the two' (Friedlander and Brown, 1974, page 220).

Another, and related, problem with the normative stance adopted by personnel management texts is that by its use of the notion of 'optimization', it skates over the difficulties underlying the implied consensus model it presents. In other words, most personnel texts do not recognize that organizations may be viewed as containing a plurality of legitimate interest groups, some of which may be antagonistic towards, and with interests incompatible to those of other groups (Fox, 1966a). Nor do they admit that the goals of individual workers and those of the organization (ignoring for a moment the confusion surrounding the use of this concept) may be persistently incompatible in the context of a market economy. After all, they would argue, a function of personnel management is to eliminate the causes of, and smooth over those manifestations of conflict which hinder the achievement of organizational goals. Such incompatibilities and conflicts that are recognized to exist, it is implied, can be contained by decision-making on the basis of 'optimization'.

But it is now a commonplace in organization theory that, generally speaking, managers do *not* seek to 'optimize' in their decision-making. For, in its literal sense, the concept of optimization rests on a figment, that of 'economic man', born of utilitarian philosophy. Economic man is assumed to (1) know every alternative available to him; (2) know the consequences of each alternative; (3) order his preferences according to his own hierarchy of values, and (4) choose from his alternatives the one that will maximize some desired value. This model of economic man, though, has been replaced by the reality of 'administrative man', who operates with a 'bounded rationality'. In other words, as Simon (1967) has pointed out, rationality is limited by the existence of many preference orders within an organization and by the decision-makers' limited knowledge (and limited

4

resources to extend this knowledge) of alternatives.[5] Because of this, decisions are reached on the basis of satisficing (i.e., finding a course of action that is just adequate or 'good enough') rather than optimizing, and within a context where organizations, instead of continually weighing ends and means, 'merely attempt to avoid uncertainty by trying to make its (*sic*) environment more subject to prediction and control' (Silverman, 1970).

Thus, the favourite expression of the texts that personnel management should aim for the 'optimum utilization of human resources in order to achieve the goals and objectives of the organization' begs the question, as both the definition and operationalization of 'optimum', in a social system of competing and incompatible interests and goals, must be problematic.

This brings us to the final difficulty with the normative stance adopted in prescriptive texts. When translated into action, even absolute normative positions are modified by context. The injunction, 'Thou shalt not kill' is waived for combat in wartime, for example. The problem personnel texts are confronted by is what interpretation should be given to their normative injunctions in different contexts. Quite apart from the difficulties, already discussed, of operationalizing the concept of optimization when a utilitarian and consensus model of the organization is not assumed, there remains the problem that even if agreement existed over the definition of the optimization injunction, its implications for appropriate *action* in different organizational and environmental contexts would vary radically.

If the problem of context affects the normative position on which these authors' prescriptions rest, it clearly has implications too for the prescriptions themselves. It is to the prescriptive area that we now turn.

Personnel texts: their prescriptive approach.   Given the vocational intent of personnel texts, they quite naturally seek to inform their readers of what the 'profession' involves, but with an emphasis on action itself (i.e., *what* properly constitutes personnel activities and *how* they should be carried out) rather than on analytical justifications for the practices they promote (i.e., *why* X activities ·are necessary or desirable, why they should be conceived of and executed in a particular way). Hence, most texts, building on the normative stance they have taken, concentrate on discussions of what constitutes 'best practice' and develop from this prescriptions for what, in their view, has to be done, and how to do it. Given management's preoccupation with day-to-day problems that have to be resolved in action, rather than with long-term conceptualization and policy-making, this emphasis is inevitable. What is often required is a blueprint for use today rather than the materials to draw one for tomorrow.

Yet, in order to provide general prescriptions, writers have tended to minimize the full extent to which different organizational and environ-

---

[5] 'Bounded rationality' has also been defined in terms particularly relevant to the argument developed later in this chapter, by Friedmann (1965): 'In short to be "bounded" means that a decision can be no more rational than the conditions under which it is made; the most that planners can hope for is the most rational decision under the circumstances.'

mental circumstances will necessitate a transformation of their general prescriptions into concrete strategy adapted to the situation in which it is to operate. In these circumstances, the inadequacy of general guidelines in helping the manager to formulate personnel policy for his organization is only too apparent. A case in point is Megginson's (1972) suggestions as to how a manager should design an overall compensation policy for his organization:

> He should select the wave theory that he believes most nearly approximates the realities of his organization. Then he should utilize it to determine the source and amount of his wage rate. (Megginson then summarizes the various wave theories such as the wage-fund theory, subsistence theory and marginal productivity theory.) After making that decision, the personnel manager will appraise the internal and external factors exerting pressure on the firm's compensation position. Probably the greatest influence today is pressure from the government in the form of laws, policies, and administrative decisions. Often these are coupled with influence from the union to raise rates. Yet a firm cannot have a policy which is much out of line with its industry or geographic area. Finally the law of supply and demand will dictate what the firm must pay while its revenue and profit position will decide what it can pay.
> The actual compensation policy and overall wage rate will be determined by the interaction of all these factors.
>
> (pages 400–401).

Quite apart from the questionable nature of some of his assertions (for example Robinson 1967, 1970; MacKay, 1971; Mace and Wilkinson, 1977, have demonstrated that 'laws' of supply and demand do *not* always dictate what the firm must pay for its labour), Megginson's level of generality is such that the manager is given very little guidance in how actually to design compensation policy at company level. How should he evaluate the various wage theories when they are based on different premises and logics? He is told, in effect, to compare like with unlike. Any theory adopted will depend both on how the manager perceives the functions of reward systems in his organization (after all the subsistence theory would run directly counter to using wage systems as an employee motivator), and which of these competing functions he considers should take priority. Payment systems, depending on how they are structured, may be used either as motivators or as a control system (Lupton and Gowler, 1972), but not as both, simultaneously, without causing confusions in logic and design. Which function the manager may plump for will depend very much on the nature of the workforce, technology, and markets with which he is involved, and which other personnel-related objectives take priority. For, the compensation policy that is primarily designed to promote harmony in industrial relations may be inappropriate if equal weight is placed on the careful control of unit labour costs.

Again, while it is sensible to say that the manager must take into consideration a range of internal and external factors likely to exert pressure on the firm's compensation position when formulating policy in this

6

area, it is of little use merely to enumerate some of the factors involved and to leave it at that. Not only does Megginson fail to suggest their likely patterns of interaction, but he does not consider what repercussions may arise from the fact that conflicting pressures may be exerted by many of these factors. For example, government intervention in incomes policy may run directly counter to union demands for higher wages, but no guidance is given as to how the manager is to weigh these conflicting claims or evaluate the type and effects of the sanctions each party may exercise, depending on the nature of other organizational and environmental circumstances. Megginson is unable to prescribe at the more micro level, at which the manager has to operate, because to do so he would need to develop *dynamic* processual models of particular organizational and environmental circumstances, as they might affect X personnel policy, given the pursuit of Y objectives, over stated time periods.

Admittedly, some of the more recent texts (e.g., Glueck, 1974) have recognized the dangers of offering prescriptions without clearly delineating the contexts in which they are to operate. In an attempt to provide some guidance in this area, Glueck attaches his prescriptions to 'seven "typical" or model' (Glueck, 1974, page 92) organizations, that are characterized along four dimensions, namely, size, technology (whether routine or non-routine), level of complexity of organization/environment, degree of volatility in organization/environment. In principle, this is a good idea, and certainly the dimensions chosen reflect the opinion of a large body of organizational theory as to what are key dimensions in explaining the effects of organizational structure on behaviour (e.g., Pugh *et al.*, 1968, 1969; Child and Mansfield, 1972; Woodward, 1965, 1970; Hickson *et al.*, 1969; Perrow, 1967a; Thompson, 1967; Zwerman, 1970; Burns and Stalker, 1961; Lawrence and Lorsch, 1967a).

But Glueck's attempt to characterize different organizational and environmental contexts along these dimensions is undermined by two major failings. First, his definitions of them are either rudimentary or nonexistent. For example, size is defined purely in terms of numbers employed, without consideration of such other size factors as net assets and market position (Pugh *et al*, 1963). Volatility is seen in terms of 'the degree to which the organization services change over time', but no reference is made to the type and nature of change involved nor to the time periods considered relevant to the measurement of the rate of different types of change. Similarly, 'complexity of organization/environment' is just defined as 'complexity of products or services', without further definition of the nature of 'complexity'. Technology is defined in terms of its being routine or non-routine, but whether Glueck is using routine in the same way as Perrow is not made clear, especially as he does not refer to the dimensions on which Perrow bases this classification, 'analyzable/unanalyzable search procedures' in response to 'variability—number of exceptions—of stimuli'. Nor is it indicated why this classification of technology was selected in

7

preference to other well-known classifications, such as those of Woodward (1965), Thompson (1967) and Hickson *et al.* (1969).[6] These are not minor quibbles, since the definitions used do in fact have implications for the type of hypotheses that are relevant to the relationships between the dimensions, quite apart from measuring and testing the extent of their validity.

The fact that Glueck did not find it necessary to make more explicit the definitions of this dimensions or the reasons for his selection of those provided (such as they are) reflects the second failing of his attempt to provide models of organizational context. Nowhere is there stated the logic behind his selection of the dimensions themselves or that behind the inter-relationships presumably implied between them. Glueck does not even explain what exactly he considers their inter-relationships might be. Hence, in practice, the organizational contexts provided are little more than clusters of ill-defined, unrelated variables awaiting the readers' knowledge of organization theory to translate them into models of organizational and environmental contexts. Because the inter-relationships between the dimensions and the logic on which they rest is never developed, Glueck can only use his 'model' organizational contexts in a very limited way. For example, when discussing which employment planning systems are appropriate to which organizational contexts, he merely writes:

> On the supply side, we look first at the extent to which the organization studies the labor market. Chances are that smaller organizations do very little here themselves; both small and medium sized organizations may contract this activity out by the use of consultants or printed matter. As far as skills inventories are concerned, smaller and medium sized organizations will have manual systems, at most. They may provide these only for subgroups of employees (management, professional or technical) that they feel are critical. Only larger organizations probably have computerized inventories.
> On the demand side, it would appear reasonable that the larger the organization, the more sophisticated the techniques, modified by the amount of change in the system. As regards where employment planning is done, it seems advantageous to formulate plans for larger, more stable organizations at headquarters, for smaller and medium sized, volatile ones at unit level, and for large, volatile organizations on both levels (page 137).

Because of the inadequacy of his model building, rather than relating particular employment planning strategies to particular contexts and explaining the logic behind the proposed match, Glueck tends to relate

[6] Hickson's paper would have been particularly helpful to Glueck in both arriving at a definition of technology, and providing a justification for his choice. In it, the authors distinguish between three types of technology concepts viz., *operations technology*—the emphasis being on the type of machinery employed and the way it is linked together, see Woodward (1965) and Thompson (1967); *materials technology*—the emphasis being on the nature of the material(s) to be processed, see Perrow (1967a) and Rushing (1968); and *knowledge technology*—(the emphasis being on the organizational processes whereby problems are analysed and dealt with, see Perrow (1967b, 1970a). For a discussion and critique of some of the posited relationships between technology, size, and organizational structure, see Donaldson (1976).

particular techniques to separate dimensions as though the organizational context concerned were unidimensional. Quite apart from the extract quoted above, this approach is clearly demonstrated by the way in which he states his 'propositions'. For example:

> Proposition 4.6   The larger the organization, the more likely it is that formal job analysis, description and specification systems will be efficient.
> Proposition 4.7   The more volatile the organization's environment, the less likely is it that detailed formal job analysis, description, and specification systems will be efficient (page 136).

Leaving aside the fact that this 'proposition' treats volatility as a property of the environment, not, as in his original definition, equally a property of the organization, this undimensional approach to organizational context leaves us with such questions as 'what then is appropriate for a large organization operating in a volatile environment?' The implied answer, a compromise, does not help to explain and weight the independent effect of each variable (size and volatility respectively), or that of their mutual interaction.

In practice, judging from his seven models of organizational context, Glueck appears to assume that his contextual variables cluster. For example, although organizations may vary in size, low level of complexity, routine technology and a low level of volatility appear to be associated, as do the converse, a high level of complexity, a non-routine technology, and a high level of volatility in the organization/environment. Thus, in his discussions, size tends to be the one distinguishing characteristic in differentiating between two basic organizational clusters. This can lead to some very obvious omissions. For example, no mention seems to be made of the independent effect of different types of technology on employment planning—a surprising omission in the light of well-known relationships between technology, the division of labour and the structure of the internal labour market (Woodward, 1965; Robinson, 1970; Doeringer and Piore, 1971), but no doubt this is due also to the rather specific sense in which he has characterized technology.

These criticisms could be applied to Glueck's use of his contextual models throughout the book and those interested to see further illustration of the inadequacies of his approach are referred in particular to the sections on 'attracting, selecting and assigning personnel', 'managerial obsolescence and development', 'financial compensation', and 'discipline and the difficult employee'.

Generally speaking, though, it is in this very inadequacy in showing practitioners how to apply the norms and prescriptions they advocate to specific contexts that personnel texts fail most notably. This criticism may now be amplified.

Personnel texts: their contextual approach.   As discussed above, personnel texts vary in the extent and the manner to which they recognize and emphasize that different organizational and environmental contexts[7] affect the design and implementation of the personnel policies they advocate. Some writers, such as Pigors and Myers and Megginson, tend to swing from descriptions of general managerial philosophies to detailed case studies without the intervention of an explicit model of organizational context that would allow for a more contingent application of the former to the latter. Others fully recognize the importance of context, when offering prescriptions for action[8] but, with the exception of Glueck whom we have already discussed, tend not to draw models of it, perhaps because, unlike Glueck, they are only too aware of the difficulties involved. Instead, other writers (Strauss and Sayles, 1960; Crichton, 1968; Miner and Miner (1973) advocate an analytical, problem-solving approach[9] that attempts to isolate what generalizations can be made 'about the behaviour of individuals, small groups, and organizations and about changes in the surrounding society', on the basis of social science research findings, and to discuss their application to the practice of management. The problem with this approach is that, in practice, acknowledgement of the importance of context seems to take the place of, and act as a substitute for, actually spelling out the implications of different contexts at the operational level.

---

[7] The term 'context' is used here in its lay sense to mean a 'general setting' or 'surrounding and connected circumstances', (see *The Penguin English Dictionary*, Second Edition, 1969). It should be pointed out that this usage is broader than that favoured by other authors: for example Pugh *et al.*, (1963) differentiated 'organizational context' (represented by the variables charter, size, resources, technology, dependence, and ownership) from the 'wider economic and cultural environment' (economic, political/ideological, social, urban/rural) and from 'organizational structure' (role and authority relationships) and 'organizational climate' (members' values, attitudes, and beliefs).

[8] See, for example, from the British literature, Anne Crichton's (1968) comment:

> What is effective personnel management? There is no easy answer to this question. What is effective for one organization may not be so for another, and what is appropriate at one stage in a company's development may be quite inappropriate at another stage and in a changed social context (page 10).

Or, from the American literature, Strauss and Sayles, (1960) comment:

> The manager needs analytical techniques that go beyond the transitory practices of specific companies at specific moments in their history. Otherwise he is limited to the rote application of techniques that may be wholly irrelevant to a wide range of problems with which he will be faced in the course of his career (page vii).

[9] See, for example, Miner and Miner (1973):

> Specific strategies must be designed, depending upon the particular task objectives and constraint structure of a given organization. The input processes, mediators, and output processes that will maximize goal attainment in one situation are unlikely to do so in another (page 46).

Or Glueck (1974):

> The administrator should follow a similar (diagnostic) model. First he needs to analyze the problem or person with a problem, looking at all the data at hand. Then he must decide what causes are operating and how the problem can be alleviated. He does not give up if the most probable cause does not seem to be operating but proceeds down the list of causes until the underlying one is found (page 6).

This is demonstrated by the way in which these authors employ their 'problem-solving' approach. Most tend to represent the foci of managerial activity as neatly packaged problems of, for example, 'manpower planning', 'appraisal and evaluation', 'wage and salary administration', 'labour relations' existing in contexts comprising checklists of 'factors to be taken into consideration' when designing policies for their solution. This approach, although an improvement on much of the earlier literature, has major deficiencies. First, in the practitioner's world, problems do not necessarily fall into such neat 'parcels' as the chapter headings would suggest (Gillespie, 1973a). For example, the problem of labour wastage is likely to reflect issues involved in 'manpower planning', 'recruitment and selection', 'wage and salary administration', and perhaps even 'industrial relations'. Second, if problems are perceived in this bounded way, it encourages the checklist approach to organizational context, as only those contextual variables relevant to the aspects of the problem that are seen from the particular functional perspective employed are considered. This has two important drawbacks. If a checklist approach is accepted as valid, there is still the difficulty of integrating several checklists if the problem is to be examined in the round. However, the utility of the checklist approach may itself be called into question. It tends to provide a static picture of context, because little indication is given of how the variables on the list interact with each other over time, existing as a dynamic context in which policy is to be designed and implemented.

Implications for action

If the dilemmas outlined above invalidate in practice the replies of personnel texts to the question 'what should be the objectives of personnel management?' at the same time they lend an air of unreality to the suggestions offered as to what activities managers should undertake to achieve these 'objectives'. Nowhere is this more apparent than when a particular technique is advocated as a means of achieving some desired end state. By way of illustration, let us look at these texts' treatment of 'management by objectives' itself.

'Management by Objectives'—the personnel texts' view. Most personnel texts mention MBO in relation to strategies for management and career development, or more specifically point to its function in 'the evaluation of individual outputs' (Miner and Miner, 1973), or in 'appraising performance' (McFarland, 1968) or even in 'using motivation to improve performance' (Megginson, 1972). Management by Objectives is generally described in terms of the participants, both superior and subordinate, having mutually analysed and agreed the key responsibilities and critical elements of the (subordinate's) job, setting mutually agreed performance objectives—in line with organizational goals—for defined periods of time, followed by an appraisal, and, possibly, a rewarding of the results achieved

at the end of the target period (see McFarland, 1968, pages 337–338; Megginson, 1972, page 679; Miner and Miner, 1973, page 190; Cuming, 1975, page 146). Most of these writers state that MBO is based on the idea of self-established role prescriptions which, arising out of a highly participative goal-setting process, are thus calculated to 'maximize individual motivation' (Miner and Miner, 1973, page 191). Cuming for example, stresses the 'Theory Y' philosophy behind MBO when he comments 'Management by Objectives is the best example of participative management—the ultimate acknowledgement of the fact that the most positive effect on morale can be obtained by allowing staff to share in management decisions which affect their destinies' (1975, page 145). The texts, as a whole, tend to see MBO as a technique in management development which combines the advantages of both motivating the employee to higher levels of performance through participative goal-setting and providing a framework for evaluating his resulting performance in terms which, superficially at least, appear more precise and quantifiable than those used in the old assessments of 'personality' and 'potential'.

Having offered up MBO as an instrument for inclusion in the manager's tool kit, most of the texts are reluctant to question whether what is claimed for it is easily achievable in practice. Some, for example Megginson (1972, page 434) and Cuming (1975, pages 155–157), are prepared to admit that care must be taken in implementation to achieve the desired results. For example, Megginson makes the point that 'the effort should be fact-oriented and as much as possible a matter of specific performance objectives, e.g., "lower the cost of production by x per cent" rather than "producing at a lower cost",' that the superior should be supportive and genuinely participative in approach, that it should be understood that experience with the technique will improve the overall quality of its use, and so on. Cuming is prepared to admit that difficulties in implementing MBO may arise if management lose 'sight of the philosophy which underpins MBO techniques' and use it to prop up existing authoritarian ideologies, or use it ritualistically, or competitively as between groups, or as a vehicle to block rather than facilitate change. The intention behind the use of MBO, he argues, is all-important: 'MBO must be seen in the context . . . of planned organizational growth which is itself clearly aimed at maintaining a participative management style' (1975, page 157). In other words, although MBO 'can be justly claimed to offer the ultimate solution to the problem of participation, because right down through the management hierarchy it emphasizes the self-control elements of taking decisions, and subsequently evaluating results, directly aimed at optimizing efficiency' (1975, page 158), this statement can stand only so long as one assumes that the management using the technique are using it on the basis of a particular philosophy.

In the reality of organizational life, this is where the rub comes. Research has indicated that, contrary to the theory, organizations often introduce

MBO as an attempt at control from above rather than as an exercise in the development of self-control (Meyer, Kay and French, 1965; Raia, 1965, 1966; Tosi and Carroll, 1968, 1970). This is not surprising as other research evidence repeatedly shows that the impetus for initiating changes in organizational strategies and techniques is often a perceived need to respond to escalating internal and external pressures (Sofer, 1961, 1964; Greiner, 1967; Dalton et al., 1970), and the case studies we have of the introduction of MBO would support this view (e.g., Wickens, 1968). If it is then perceived by the participants as an externally imposed and potentially punishment-centred control mechanism, as in the case of other control systems (such as incentive payment systems), they are likely to circumvent its intentions. If there is a wide measure of resistance or apathy in the organization, this may be done by collusion, so that at junior and middle management levels at least, MBO dissolves 'into a ritualistic form-filling exercise' (Molander, 1972, page 79), which nobody takes seriously. Alternatively, individuals may choose to 'work the system' by what has been termed 'suboptimization' (Bryan, 1966), in order to achieve personal goals at the expense of the organizational objectives whose achievement MBO is supposed to facilitate. This operates in two main forms: the manager may deliberately select a goal he knows he can achieve, simple rather than complex, and readily quantifiable, or he may deliberately avoid selecting high risk but potentially rewarding programmes in favour of maintaining the system as it is.

Further, it is exactly in those situations in which MBO is most likely to be seized upon—when the organization is suffering internal and/or market pressure—that, because resources are short and remaining slack is disappearing there are likely to exist tensions and competition between individuals and groups, which may be exacerbated by their struggle to achieve specified standards that are potentially incompatible. Molander quotes a typical example, 'a sales manager may be recommended to introduce Y new products in a given period, and the production manager to increase his production by X per cent' (1972, page 77). He adds 'since the introduction of new products will initially involve loss of production there is likely to be conflict' (1972, pages 77–78). The problems involved in co-ordinating and integrating effort directed at functional goal achievement under MBO schemes may also exacerbate existing staff-line conflict, as when, for example, a staff manager is set targets agreed by his superior, which cannot be attained without the cooperation of line colleagues outside his control.

Again, the pressures that lead to a desire to 'tighten up the organization' may arise out of organizational and environmental circumstances that themselves hinder the implementation of an MBO scheme. As Wickens (1968) points out, firms engaged in unit and small batch production, operating in variable and often unpredictable market conditions, have the problem that planning can only be done for a short time span. In these circumstances, an MBO programme is likely to succeed only if long-term overall objectives are rather loose, and if departmental and sectional objectives, apart from being highly integrated, are kept flexible and frequently revised (cf., Lindblom, 1959). Yet, in such organizations, Wickens argues, objectives have little relevance unless they are broken down and re-applied at every level—'yet the short term nature of the planning cycle, the frequent changes of situation, and the complex inter-departmental relationships make this a very difficult and time consuming task' (1968, page 372). At the same time, the usefulness of MBO is somewhat restricted because 'as performance will have been greatly affected by many factors outside the manager's control . . . performance appraisal in terms of the achievement of predetermined objectives is necessarily highly subjective' (1968, page 372). Conversely, Wickens indicates why the market situation and technology employed facilitate the introduction (and potential utility) of MBO into organizations with a mass production or process technology.

The failure of many personnel texts is not that they do not recognize that problems may arise in implementing MBO—Cuming goes out of his way to mention the major difficulties involved and even Megginson devotes a sentence to 'disadvantages'—but they do not spell out under *which organizational and environmental circumstances* specific problems are likely to arise, nor the submerged implications of such patterns of behaviour. Thus, for example, although Cuming lays most of the difficulties in, and dysfunctions arising out of, the implementation of MBO at the door of inappropriate managerial philosophies, he does not go on to explain *why*, in certain circumstances, if introduced, MBO will inevitably become a vehicle for authoritarian management. It is not sufficient merely to suggest what factors are likely to prove incompatible with the successful implementation of MBO (e.g., authoritarian management), but necessary to ask

1. what *configurations* of organizational/environmental circumstances make it difficult or inappropriate to implement MBO;
2. are these circumstances open to change, and what are the costs, in other areas, of attempting such changes;
3. what should be the strategies to change those factors that it is considered both feasible and desirable to change in order to achieve successful implementation.

These questions have to be asked if the manager is to be in a position to decide not just whether and how to introduce successful MBO, but whether the potential costs involved to achieve this make the exercise worthwhile overall. Put another way, questions need to be asked that will enable the manager to see MBO (or any other technique for that matter) in a much broader context than most of the textbooks envisage.

When such questions are not posed, personnel texts tend to take two false turnings. First, solutions are offered to overcome problems that really beg the question. For example, in relation to one of the potential dysfunctions of MBO, that it may exacerbate group conflict as different groups strive to achieve desirable but basically incompatible goals, it is often suggested that this may be overcome by targets being set on an inter-group basis, with superiors of different functions agreeing together mutually compatible targets for their own function (Cuming, 1975, page 157). What is not questioned is whether or not, if this takes place, interfunctional conflict will merely be transferred to a higher level in the organization and acted out in another arena where more insidious political pressures might also be operating (Lupton, 1975a). Nor is it questioned to what extent group target setting alternatively might lead to a dilution of effort as, to reach agreement, targets embrace the lowest common denominator, or are stated in sufficiently loose terms as to skate over potential conflict, or to allow for further bargaining and negotiation elsewhere. In addition, returning to our dominant theme, this literature does not suggest what configuration of organizational/environmental circumstances is likely to produce which of these hypothesized reactions to group target setting. No doubt the authors have relevant ideas about conflict or decision-making that are discussed elsewhere in their texts, but because of their bounded 'topic' rather than true problem-solving approach (albeit their assertions to the contrary), no reference is made to how knowledge in these areas can be used to achieve a more sophisticated analysis and more adequate solutions to the issue in hand.

Second, this restricted approach to the evaluation of techniques offered in the literature encourages the student to acquire an inadequate perspective towards managerial practice. Because techniques are placed in an inadequate contextual framework, the emphasis tends to be less on how X technique can contribute to the solution of Y problem in Z context, and more on the technique as an end in itself. Thus, more attention is directed to what an MBO programme consists of, and the different stages that have to be implemented, than to what it can or cannot achieve, and the reasons why, in different organizational contexts. Given this approach, it is not surprising that McFarland (1967) found in his study of the personnel function that personnel specialists, in practice, abandoned the attempt to examine their activities in terms of organizational ends and instead came to consider the programmes that they were involved in designing and executing as ends in themselves.

The problem restated

This chapter opened with the suggestion that students entering and managers exercising the personnel management functions were interested in two main questions—what should be the objectives of personnel management, and how could these best be achieved. In the following sections, it was suggested that many of the texts, designed to help managers answer these questions, not only failed to do so, but at times were positively unhelpful. This stems basically from two failings. First, through their confused treatment of organizational goals, the texts state personnel objectives in terms that raise more questions than they answer. This ultimately confuses much of what they have to say about the nature of the personnel function itself as, in very real terms, a statement of personnel objectives is a statement about how an organization defines its personnel function or, at best, perceives its responsibilities and priorities. Second, through their neglect of context, the prescriptive intention of these books succumbs to stilted generalizations that neglect both the complexities and dynamism of real organizations.

If more attention was paid to context, however, it would become clear that the student's and manager's two questions might be restated in terms of one dominant preoccupation: What is it *feasible* for the personnel function to do in a particular organization/environment, quite apart from what might be agreed to be necessary or desirable? For, in practice, what the personnel function *should* do and how it *should* do it often takes second place to what it is *able* to undertake and in what way, in the particular context in which it operates. Thus, whether policy is feasible or not depends not only on the appropriateness of its design, in the light of specific organizational contexts and objectives, but on the *degree of power that context affords those who have designed the policy to implement it.* These two factors are, of course, inter-related. No amount of advocacy of policy based on 'best practice', even if appropriate to organizational circumstances and requirements, will alter the nature of personnel practice in companies if the managers responsible for implementing such policy lack the power to do so. Equally, of course, attempts to implement irrelevant or inappropriate 'best practice' may further diminish what authority is possessed by those exercising the personnel function. Organizational context includes the power relationships in which the personnel manager is involved, just as much as those 'external' conditions for which he has to plan and to which he has to adapt. The question of power, neglected in much of the personnel management literature, needs to be considered before normative and prescriptive injunctions are made. Personnel objectives at any point in time have to take into consideration the political realities of organizational behaviour that circumscribe any manager's ability to pursue desired courses of action. In these circumstances, it is not surprising that what is defined as an objective often represents no more than what the manager thinks *can* be done rather than what he thinks *ought* to be done.

Hence, the two questions personnel managers start by asking, the 'ought' questions, cannot be considered independently from the much neglected 'can' questions. Indeed, the former often gets lost sight of, as managers settle for what is practicable if not ideal. In contrast, what is intended in this book is to explore the relationships between these two types of question, to consider how the personnel manager *can* achieve what *should* be appropriate personnel management objectives in particular organizational contexts.

But before embarking on this central issue, some preliminary questions need to be considered. Namely, what exactly *is* the personnel function to which we have been loosely referring? What are the bases of power and legitimacy in organizations that are theoretically available to its managers? In practice, what influence in policy formulation and implementation has this function enjoyed in the recent past? Chapter 2 will consider the first two questions, while the following chapter, based on recent case-study data, will examine the third, perhaps most revealing, question.

2. The personnel function: power and authority

How much power and authority does the personnel function possess? What at first sight might appear a relatively straightforward question rapidly loses its simplicity when, on reflection, it becomes apparent that the three concepts involved, namely 'function', 'power', and 'authority', are problematic. Moreover, if the unspoken rider is added, 'in different organizational contexts', the question becomes even less straightforward. So, before attempting an answer, what is meant by the concepts involved must be considered.

The personnel function: a definition

Superficially, a definition of the personnel management function can be easily supplied: it is that aspect of an organization that exercises 'personnel' management, that is concerned with the motivation and control of employees, for the achievement of specified objectives. Yet, this sort of definition falls into the same trap as the textbooks' one of personnel management objectives. It says all and nothing. For on closer examination, the very label 'personnel' 'management' 'function' contains ambiguities and incompatibilities. For example, 'function' can have several meanings. Quite apart from its mathematical and sociological usage,[1] managers use

[1] In mathematics, for example, when it is said that phenomenon X is a function of phenomenon Y, it is meant that X varies in proportion as does Y. When used in its sociological sense, for example, 'low absenteeism is a function of good personnel management', it refers to a diagnosed objective consequence which a social phenomenon has for a wider system of which it is a part. These two definitions are related. As Mitchell writes:

Cont. next page

the term in two distinct, yet overlapping senses. Taking its basic meaning to indicate 'something of the nature of specialization in contribution or activity' (Thomason, 1975, page 13), personnel 'function' can refer either to an *activity* (by implication arising from the system's/organization's need) or to that activity's *institutionalized* or *departmental presence* within the organization, in this case the *personnel department.*

Thus, while some writers, for example, McFarland (1968) and Lyons (1971)[2] are at pains to make clear the distinction between the personnel function proper and its institutionalized presence, the personnel department, others use the term to refer interchangeably to either department or function. For example, reference is made to the fact that the 'personnel function will no longer be able to justify itself to top management by citing numbers or listing activities' (Richardson, 1968) or 'personnel management has generally been considered, in traditional terms, a staff function ... in actual practice, however, this limitation upon the authority vested in the personnel function is often not nearly as pronounced as the staff designation would seem to imply' (Miner and Miner, 1973), and so on. In practice, of course, the 'personnel department' and the 'personnel function' although not co-terminous are not fully discrete either and this exacerbates the confusion. If we can accept for the moment the traditional if simplistic definition of the personnel function as an activity (i.e., as the optimum utilization of human resources in pursuit of organizational goals), we can see that *as an activity* it must be necessarily spread beyond the confines of the personnel department and involve managers of other 'functions' whether production, marketing, finance, and so on. As Megginson writes, 'management is personnel management, because all managers are involved with human factors in varying degrees ... line management cannot divest itself of the responsibility for the personnel administration function by appointing staff and functional executives to be responsible for it' (1972, page 55).

[2] As when McFarland states:

> Whether it is explicitly recognized or not an employee relations function exists in every organization. Making the function more systematic by identifying it as a managerial responsibility is based on the fact that for most companies the cost of its human resources is one of the biggest categories of costs it faces (1968, page 4).

Or Lyons:

> Personnel management is that part of the function of management that arises out of the fact that an enterprise has to use people ... this definition helps to show that the personnel function exists quite independently of whether specialists are employed or not (1971, pages 1–2).

Footnote 1 (cont.)

> This is because function as consequence for the state of the system implies that all social phenomena in a system are thought, at least initially, to be relevant to a consideration of its persistence. It is then but a short step to postulating that all phenomena in a system are inter-related and that a change in one area of a social system will have ramifications throughout the system. Thus function as consequence and function as related variation are often closely connected' (1968, page 81).

This confusion is further reflected in common definitions of what comprises personnel management. Whatever their stated intention, some appear to be referring to the function *in toto*, while others to its departmental presence alone. The 'functional' definitions all run along similar lines. Compare that of the IPM (1963) with that of Pigors and Myers (1969), Megginson (1972), Glueck (1974), and Jucius (1975).

IPM (1963)
Personnel management is a responsibility of all those who manage people, as well as being a description of the work of those who are employed as specialists. It is that part of management which is concerned with people at work and with their relationships within an enterprise. Personnel management aims to achieve both efficiency and justice, neither of which can be pursued successfully without the other. It seeks to bring together and develop into an effective organization the men and women who make up an enterprise, enabling each to make his own best contribution to its success both as an individual and as a member of a working group. It seeks to provide fair terms and conditions of employment, and satisfying work for those employed.

Pigors and Myers (1969)
Since management aims at getting effective results *with people*, personnel administration is a basic management function or activity permeating all levels of management in any organization. ... Personnel administration is ... organizing and treating individuals at work so that they will get the greatest possible realization of their intrinsic abilities, thus attaining maximum efficiency for themselves and their group, and thereby giving the enterprise of which they are a part its determining competitive advantage and its optimum results.

Megginson (1972)
It is believed that the most significant aspect of personnel management is to be found through the direction and control of the human resources of an organization in its daily operations ... the successful performance of the personnel function necessitates that each manager orient himself within his total business environment in order to help achieve the various organizational programs and objectives.

Glueck (1974)
Basically personnel is concerned with the matching of people to the jobs that must be done to achieve the organization's goals.

Jucius (1975)
Personnel management is defined here as follows: The field of management which has to do with planning, organizing, directing and controlling the functions of procuring, developing, maintaining and utilizing a labor force, such that the
(a) Objectives for which the company is established are attained economically and effectively.
(b) Objectives of all levels of personnel are served to the highest possible degree.
(c) Objectives of society are duly considered and served.

In terms of these definitions, the function of personnel management is to obtain the optimum utilization of human resources for the achievement of organizational goals, while at the same time providing opportunities for these human resources to attain an equitable reward for their efforts and an opportunity for some measure of self-fulfilment within the organization. The potential conflict here, as indicated in the previous chapter, can give rise to further ambiguities in pinning down exactly what the function comprises and this problem will be returned to later.

Alternatively, some definitions of what comprises personnel management appear to centre on those activities undertaken by personnel specialists within a formal personnel department, to the exclusion of those 'personnel activities that are the responsibility of all management'. Compare the 'departmental' definitions of Miner and Miner (1973), Glueck (1974) and Cuming (1975) with the 'functional' definitions quoted above.

Miner and Miner (1973)
Personnel management may be defined as involving the development, application, and evaluation of policies, procedures, methods, and programs relating to the individual in the organization.

Glueck (1974)
Personnel administration is that function of any work organization concerned with providing for its human resources. It involves planning for human resource needs, finding and hiring employees, training and compensating them, and finally retiring them.

Cuming (1975)
Personnel management is concerned with obtaining the best possible staff for an organization and, having got them, looking after them so that they will want to stay and give of their best to their jobs.

All these definitions are concerned less with the function of personnel management, in its sociological sense, or even with the personnel function in its correct managerial sense, and more with those activities undertaken by the specialist personnel department. As such, they generally go on to list what they term the *content* of personnel management, which is usually seen to involve such specialist activities as organizational planning, manpower planning, job analysis, recruitment and selection, appraisal and evaluation, training, management development, wages and salary administration, job evaluation, industrial relations, discipline, safety, counselling, and 'welfare'.

Ambiguities. To summarize, a clear answer to the question 'what is the personnel management function?' cannot be given due to the ambiguous usage of the term 'function' itself. 'Function', in its sociological sense, can refer to outcomes of the personnel management process (e.g., 'lack of strike action was a function of our personnel management'), and as such represents a purely positive statement. Yet, this 'function' of personnel management may be an outcome of the personnel 'function', in its precise managerial sense (i.e., an outcome of the optimum utilization of human resources to achieve organizational goals), or an outcome of activities of the personnel 'function', meaning the personnel department. Of these two meanings of 'function', the first represents a normative statement of what the activity or process *should* comprise. The second, confusing the issue still further, can refer to two different perspectives on the personnel department. It can refer to those specialist personnel activities that in the view of the commentator *should* be the responsibility of a personnel department (again a normative stance), or to those that the department actually undertakes (a positive perspective).

Quite apart from the misunderstandings generated by this definitional confusion, each definition contains within it some of the major ambiguities that beset personnel management. First, there is the problem of establishing that any outcome is the direct function (in its sociological sense) of personnel management. The nature of the raw materials of personnel management, the human resource, is such that it cannot be shielded from extraorganizational influences to the same extent as other resources employed, once within the organization's boundaries. Moreover, it is both reactive and proactive, and cannot be manipulated as easily as an inanimate object. As a factor in production, less is known about what makes individuals function optimally and less control may be exercised over their behaviour, than in the case of machinery or even capital. Hence, there are problems in establishing direct links of causation between managerial activities and employee behaviour. Is a decrease in labour turnover, for example, due to management improving working conditions, or due to adverse conditions in the local labour market, or, at the individual level, to the employee's refusal to look for jobs outside his immediate locality, due to his unwillingness to cause disruption in his domestic life! Given that each individual human resource may place a different emphasis on these different factors (or be influenced by yet other considerations in his decision to leave or stay), it is difficult to evaluate whether or to what extent personnel management policies in fact do have the function of reducing the labour turnover of a particular group of workers. This difficulty of establishing direct causal relationships between personnel activities and desired outcomes contributes to the ambiguity surrounding personnel management. On the one hand, some commentators regard it as perhaps the most crucial and pervasive of all managerial activities upon whose success all the others ultimately depend[3] while others, having difficulty in measuring the results of personnel management as a specialist activity, speak of a 'kind of generalized inferiority complex (that) pervades the personnel field' (Herman, 1968, page 25).

[3] See, for example, the comment of L. B. Neumiller, Chairman of Caterpillar Tractor Co., quoted in Herman '(personnel work) is very close to the heart of the business . . . No business can achieve its true destiny unless its management is properly employee centred' (1968, page 20).

This ambiguity—over their inability to prove a direct relationship between personnel management activities and outcomes on the one hand, yet on the other, the conviction that personnel management, being a component of all managerial activities, is central to the achievement of organizational success—is a reflection of another ambiguity arising out of the definitional problems already discussed. Much of the personnel function, as the activity of optimally utilizing human resources, is necessarily in the hands of line management (or other staff managers in so far as they have executive responsibilities) who themselves have to work through people to achieve their objectives. For example, much of the day-to-day administration of wage payment systems is in the hands of first line supervision, as is the monitoring, control and sanctioning of casual absenteeism, and the organization of training. In contrast, the personnel function as a specialist department is chiefly concerned with providing a framework to facilitate the acquisition, development, and retention of efficient human inputs for use within other functional systems, such as production, marketing, and so on. Thus, the personnel function, as an activity, is dependent on the personnel function, as a specialist department, for its success. For it is the department that supplies the right (or wrong) quality and quantity of human resources and which designs many of the systems whereby this resource is retained and its efficiency optimized. Yet the department is equally dependent on the manner in which the personnel function is carried out elsewhere in the organization, for its ability to undertake its specialist activities successfully. For instance, if line managers wish to have complete freedom of action in, say, operating existing wage payment systems, or in settling industrial relations disputes, or in allocating labour, and refuse to work within the infrastructures designed by the specialist department, the work of the latter is undermined. This, in turn, may feedback on to line management's ability to practise efficient personnel management. In other words, just as at the conceptual level the definition of function causes confusion due to its multi-faceted nature, so at the operational level the different facets of the personnel function remain ambiguous due to the interactive and overlapping nature of different activities, carried out in different parts of the organization, but all nominally under the collective title of personnel management.

The third ambiguity that confronts personnel management is implicit in the definition of the function as an activity. Referring back, in particular, to those of the IPM, Pigors and Myers, and of Jucius, it can be seen that the goals of personnel management are stated in terms of both organizational efficiency and individual development and self-fulfilment. In practice, it cannot be automatically assumed that these two objectives are mutually compatible in organizations which, even if not profit-maximizing, are certainly cost-conscious. The assumptions that are often implicit in the achievement of short-term efficiency (e.g., a high division of labour and the development of semi-skilled short-cycle, repetitive jobs, a tightly reciprocal relationship between effort and reward, labour an expendable overhead at times of economic recession), may run directly counter to the hopeful philosophy of Megginson that 'the efficiency and effectiveness of employee productivity results from the recognition of, and enhancement of, the human dignity of each individual employee' (1972, page 20).

Thomason (1975) has shown clearly how these two potentially incompatible orientations, what might be called the 'personnel' and the 'management' approaches to the function, have arisen. The personnel manager's concern with the efficient utilization of human resources in pursuit of organizational goals, as he points out, represents his acceptance of the classical managerial position. In other words, the view that managers, as agents of the owners or shareholders, are engaged to organize, direct, and control the necessary resources, including people, to achieve those organizational ends desired by the latter. Leaving aside the conceptual difficulties that arise from this statement, concerning means/ends relationships and the separation of ownership and control, and accepting it at face value, a personnel manager who accepts this definition of management must ultimately commit himself to an employer's perspective in carrying out his managerial activities, and align himself closely 'with the general managerial control function' (Thomason, 1975, page 18). This orientation to personnel management is, of course, invariably adopted by managers in other functional areas when acting out the personnel functions involved in their own managerial activities (McCaig, 1976).

On the other hand, there exists a different conception of personnel management, rooted in its historical development as a specialist activity. This is the view that because the major resource of personnel management, viz., people, is of a different order to other resources, when working as specialists in this function, their orientation should not be exclusively managerial. It is argued that, compared with other managerial roles, that of the personnel management specialist is 'different in that it has to serve not only the employer, but also act in the interests of employees as individual human beings and, by extension, the interests of society' (Miller, 1959, page 92). In other words, the personnel manager should mediate between workers and employers, representing the interests of each party to the other. Concern for the workers' lot in the early twentieth century and the development of the welfare officer role, combined with that of 'the custodian of the corporate conscience' (Miller, 1959, page 91) arose out of what Thomason (1975) has rightly described as a Christian, authoritarian paternalism. This tradition received a major boost from the human relations movement when, to supplement the Quaker tradition of welfare, the gospel was preached that concern for workers as people requiring a measure of self-fulfilment would mean greater efficiency and lower costs. Ideas of efficiency through managerial control and concern for the lot of the workers came together as the human relations movement asserted the feasibility of a form of control through motivation.

24

Similarly, in practice if not in theory, control through welfare became a means, particularly in America, of excluding the independent organization of workers by 'keeping the unions out' (Myers, 1976). The improvement of the worker's lot was encouraged, if he would recognize the provisions made for him as privileges accorded by a generous, if paternalistic, management, not as rights won in challenge of the managerial prerogative. Clearly, as Thomason points out, this approach to industrial relations of warding off potential collective organization, through the paternalistic and authoritarian welfare provision, has, over the years, diminished considerably.

> The early resisters of trade union pressures were turned by the tide of union development into what became known as fire-fighters. Their role became not one of merely dealing with worker/union troubles when they appeared (pure fire-fighting) but of seeking to impose procedural constraints upon the workers' organizations so that the difficulties could be contained as far as possible (Thomason, 1975, page 24).

The aim of personnel management, though, remained the same: to retain, if not extend, the scope of managerial control through 'improving management's chances of winning the battles with trade unions over prerogatives and rights' (Thomason, 1975, page 26).

As Thomason concludes:

> ... if we see personnel management as having developed from two diverse origins, the one paternalistically orientated towards the welfare of the employees and the other rationally derived from corporate needs to control, we have a foundation for understanding the ambivalence so often associated with the function. This is reinforced in practice by the possibility of using similar methods to serve very different ends: a joint consultative committee might be established either to improve communication for the benefit of all involved, or to provide a barrier to the further development of independent associations of employees. Practically any activity which is or has been associated with the personnel manager's role could be characterized in each of these ways (Thomason, 1975, page 26).

In these circumstances, it is not surprising that both the personnel function proper and its institutionalized presence, the personnel department, often lack a clear sense of direction and purpose. A recent research study, for example, found:

> ... that the role of the personnel department was not clearly defined. There was a lack of clear definition in management's expectations of the personnel function, and a corresponding reticence among personnel managers to indicate what they felt this role should be. The authors of the report felt that the unclear definition of personnel responsibilities was the root of many of the problems found in the personnel department. This lack of definition applied to the purpose of the personnel function, the relationship of the personnel function to line management, and the relationship to other departments on personnel matters (Ritzer and Trice, 1969, page 65).

It may be argued that this confusion, arising from the ambiguities surrounding the function, is further reflected, to quote Drucker, in the 'hodge-podge' of activities that personnel departments often undertake. Thus, he comments:

> Personnel administration . . is largely a collection of incidental techniques without much internal cohesion. As personnel administration conceives the job of managing worker and work, it is partly a file clerk's job, partly a housekeeping job, partly a social worker's job and partly fire-fighting to head off union trouble or to settle it . . . the things the personnel administrator is typically responsible for—safety and pension plans, the suggestion system, the employment office and union's grievances—are necessary chores. I doubt though that they should be put together in one department for they are a hodge-podge . . . They are neither one function by kinship of skills required to carry out the activities, nor are they one function by being linked together in the work process, by forming a distinct stage in the work of the managers or in the process of the business (Drucker, 1961, pages 269–270).

Summary. From this discussion it can be seen that defining the personnel function is no easy task. Ambiguities in definition generate confusion at the operational level about the nature and locus of personnel management responsibilities, which in turn promotes a lack of coherence in the allocation of personnel activities, and gives rise to critical assessments of the function. But, is Drucker's assessment, echoed by other commentators (Crichton, 1968; Herman, 1968; McFarland, 1968) still true of the 1970s? If it is, it would appear likely that these self-reinforcing ambiguities and confusions might have important implications for the levels of power and influence managers are able to command when attempting to design and implement personnel strategy, or even when seeking to gain acceptance for a personnel management point of view in other areas of decision-making. However, before turning to this question in the next chapter, it may be useful to consider briefly what we mean by power, and to reflect on how it is obtained.

Power in organizations

What exactly is power? Most writers follow Dahl's (1957) definition that power is something that a person A has over someone else B, 'to the extent that he can get B to do something B would not otherwise do'. More precisely, it has been defined as a 'causal relation between the preferences of an actor regarding an outcome and the outcome itself' (Nagel, 1975). Either way, power is someone's—or the group's he represents—*capability* of exercising *influence* over the attitudes and/or behaviour of other individuals or groups. How do they achieve this capability? And in what circumstances? Generally speaking, the answer appears to be in the relationship between the properties, or potential power bases available to groups and individuals and their skills in matching these with the motivational bases of those they wish to influence. In other words, in order to exert influence, a group or individual must possess or control something (e.g., status, money, information, knowledge) that is valued by, and is salient, at that time and in that place, to those they wish to influence. If it meets these conditions, then a resource may be considered an actual power base. Clearly, though, power is therefore a contingent, not an absolute commodity. Bearing this in mind, let us consider first how specialist functions or departments gain power and influence.

Power bases of functional groups. At the group or departmental level, the arguments presented by Hickson *et al.*, (1971) are central to an explanation of power in organizations. Briefly, they run as follows. The authors suggest that organizations can be viewed as open systems of inter-dependent specialized functions or sub-units whose major task is to cope with uncertainties, whether environmentally or internally generated, that may impede survival or growth. It is in this coping with uncertainty[4] and the resulting imbalance of reciprocal interdependence among the sub-units, that power relations among them is generated. For, following Emerson (1962), they argue that as dependency in a social relationship is the reverse of power, so conversely a department's/sub-unit's power may be said to reside in its ability to maintain its relative autonomy[5] while increasing the dependence of other such units upon its capacity, ex-clusively, to fulfil their requirements.[6] Hence, if a department is regarded as highly *central*[7] (in the degree to which, or the speed and severity with which its activities can affect those of other departments and the final outputs of the organization), if its coping activities are seen as both highly *expert* and *non-substitutable*,[8] then, it is suggested, it will have power, due to other departments' dependency on it for the achievement of their own

---

[4] Many writers have suggested that the ability of different groups in organizations to cope with uncertainty, whether generated externally or internally, is their basis of power. See, for example, Crozier (1964); Perrow, (1961, 1970a); Lawrence and Lorsch (1967a).

[5] This autonomy can be only *relative*, for as Hickson *et al.* state, functional units within organizations are not free to opt out altogether. Thus, 'the essence of an organization is limitation of the autonomy of all its members or parts; since all are subject to power from others; for sub-units, unlike individuals, are not free to make a decision to participate . . . nor to decide whether or not to come together in political relationships. They must. They exist to do so' (1971, page 217).

[6] Cf. Emerson's suggestion that 'the dependence of actor A upon actor B is (1) directly proportional to A's motivational investment in goals mediated by B, and (2) inversely proportional to the availability of those goals to A outside the A-B relation' (1962, page 32).

[7] A unit's centrality may be based on various factors. It may comprise a high level of workflow pervasiveness (defined as the degree to which the workflows of a sub-unit connect with the workflows of other sub-units) or of workflow immediacy (defined as the speed and severity with which the workflows of a sub-unit affect the final outputs of the organization).

[8] Cf., Mechanic's hypothesis that 'other factors remaining constant, a person difficult to replace will have greater power than a person easily replaceable' (1962, page 352). Also Dubin's comment that 'for any given level of functional importance in an organization, the power residing in a functionary is inversely proportional to the number of other functionaries in the organization capable of performing the function' (1963, page 21).

objectives and, at the individual level, for the rewards associated with such an achievement (Hickson *et al.*, 1971). Conversely, this power is likely to be diminished if organizational or environmental factors operate to lower the department's saliency for previously dependent groups. For example, routinization, by preventing uncertainty (e.g., through long-term supply contracts, or planned maintenance) or by decreasing the level of expertise required to cope with it, (e.g., standard procedures of diagnosis and sequences of appropriate remedies that enable nurses to substitute for doctors in emergencies), thus lowering both centrality and substitutability, can decrease a department's power.

This discussion provides a useful starting point in considering why different functions either possess or lack power and why a particular function's level of power may vary as between organizations,[9] for the question of context, through such concepts as centrality, substitutability, and uncertainty, is highlighted rather than ignored. In other words, Hickson *et al.* suggest that a function's power will depend on the opportunities its organizational context provides for it to cope with uncertainties whose resolution is essential to the organization's survival and growth. As will be discussed in subsequent chapters, recent changes in organizational context (in terms of legislation, employee expectations, developments in technological and economic environments, and so on) have paved the way for the personnel function to increase its power through its ability to cope with areas of uncertainty which, until recently, did not exist, or were not perceived as critical to organizational success.

However, this theory of power does leave several questions unresolved—mainly about how it is obtained in the first place. To argue that a department's power lies in its ability to control 'strategic contingencies' (or uncertainties) is to explain sources of power, at departmental level, in terms of structural relationships. But where did the department get the power initially to establish this control? Indeed, control of 'strategic contingencies' might reasonably be seen as a consequence of existing power, whereby the 'ruling coalitions' structure both organizational and environmental relationships, through the exercise of 'strategic choice', in such a way as to reinforce their position (Cyert and March, 1963; Perrow, 1970b; Child, 1972). For, as Clegg has pointed out:

> Once we allow that some members of organizations may be in a position to choose the environment in which they operate, then the emphasis on the determining features of the environment diminishes. It might be that the home market is less variable than the export market, and it might be that members who manage exports are more 'strategically contingent', and hence by definition of

[9] Cf., Woodward's (1965) finding that unit, large batch and mass, and process production each appear to have a critical function (e.g., development in unit and small batch, production in large batch and mass production, marketing in process production) of key importance to the organization's overall growth and survival, and that managers working in their organization's critical function were considered its élite.

the theory, more powerful, than these other members. This would tell us little if the crucial and unconsidered question is *who* chose to export, and how and why they chose to (1975, pages 45–46).[10]

But, if it is accepted that some individuals within a functional sub-unit can choose and make decisions for it, another circularity in defining the basis of power emerges. To speak of a sub-unit, which presumably is a collective of various and, possibly, at times, conflicting interests, as one 'thing', is to recognize that some of its members have the power to speak for it. Where does *their* power come from? The question of how individual's *within groups* come to possess power will be considered shortly but, having pointed out this dilemma, what alternative explanation of departmental power can be offered?

What is suggested here, is that while power certainly results from the development of strategic structural relationships, this development is either facilitated or impeded by existing norms and values that accord different groups and individuals a greater or lesser capacity to exploit situations. An analogy may be drawn with a game of chess, in which pieces gain their power, not only through their current positions (as in the theory just discussed), but through the rules of the game which accord some pieces a more privileged position, with a wider range of potential moves, to start with (Clegg, 1975). Compare, for example, the position of the Queen with that of the pawn or, for that matter, that of the Board of a company with, say, its work study department. What then are the sources of these taken-for-granted rules that underwrite some departments' influence attempts, or power seeking behaviours, as more legitimate and hence potentially more successful, than those of others? On this there seems to be a wide measure of agreement: such rules arise from the 'dominant ideology' (Allen, 1975), or the values encapsulated in the 'dominant process of material reproduction' in the society in which the organizations exist (Whitley, 1975). In capitalist society these tend to the utililarian values, ultimately expressed in financial terms.

This brings the argument back to issues raised earlier in this chapter. In discussing the common definition of the personnel function as 'the optimization of human resources in the pursuit of organizational goals', the point was made that organizational goals are hard to pin down and, in practice, rarely take the optimizing form of 'highest profitability/return on capital compatible with long-term stability and growth' that in managerial writing is often implied (see, for example, Miner and Miner, 1973, page 7). However, bearing this in mind, it is argued that in industrial organizations, although the values of capitalism may possibly be expressed in these terms in their formal 'public charters', in practice such values are implemented in

[10] It is interesting, in the light of this critique, that many of the contextual changes that have provided opportunities for the personnel function to increase its power have been government imposed and, hence, relatively immune from the manipulative influences to which Clegg refers.

a modified form through the more limited *success criteria* used to judge organizational, departmental, and managerial performance.

If this is so, a department/function's ability to achieve organizational power may be restated as follows:

1. Groups establish and maintain power through their control of 'strategic contingencies' (i.e., through their exclusive ability to cope with uncertainties whose resolution is generally accepted as vital to organizational survival and growth and, as such, is valued by other groups in the organization).
2. Their chances of gaining control of these contingencies, and the likelihood that those they can cope with will be labelled as strategic, is determined by pre-existing ground rules that arise out of the dominant social values.
3. At organizational level, these values are expressed in terms of the success criteria used to measure performance throughout the organization.

Hence the powerful management functions are likely to be those that can show that their success criteria are closely aligned to those of the organization as a whole, which in turn are legitimized through their match with the dominant social ideology. This proposition will be developed in subsequent chapters. However, it may be noted at this point that any change in the dominant social ideology, for example, a move from utilitarian to non-utilitarian, humanistic values, is likely to give rise to different types of success criteria and, in so doing, present opportunities for previously non-influential groups to gain power. Recent changes of this nature have offered such opportunities to the personnel function, and such developments will be discussed later.

Having said this, it remains to consider briefly how individual managers themselves achieve power within these units, as ultimately it is they who are likely to negotiate a department's control of strategic contingencies and exercise the resulting power in organizational policy-making and implementation.

Individual power and authority. How is it that within a function some individuals clearly have more authority and exercise more influence than others? It is a commonplace that, within a management group, some junior managers appear to influence decision-making to a far greater extent than their formal position would suggest (the 'high flyers'), while in other cases, a manager nominally senior to his colleagues may appear to be consistently overridden in group decision-making. What then are the sources of power for individuals in organizations? (French and Raven, 1960; Cartwright, 1965).

First, as at departmental level, an individual's 'singular possession of a valued area of technical competence' (Pettigrew, 1976, page 196), some scarce and sought after skill or knowledge, can be a source of *expert* power to him, as it may create dependency on him in others. As Blau puts it:

> By supplying services in demand to others, a person establishes power over them. If he regularly renders needed services they cannot readily obtain elsewhere, others become dependent on and obligated to him for these services, unless they in turn can supply services to the former person that he needs. The power of one individual over another thus depends on the social alternatives or lack of them available to the subjected individual (1964, page 118).

This is basically Emerson's argument that Hickson *et al.* applied at the functional unit level in his discussion of substitutability and centrality. Related to this source of power is the individual's ability to control information through a process of collecting, filtering and, ultimately, reformulating it. Those occupying roles of high boundary relevance (i.e., roles that involve many significant work contacts across departmental or organizational boundaries) are particularly well placed to take advantage of this source of power.

Both these sources of power are available to those whose formal position in their department is still relatively junior. In fact, it may be precisely because they are junior that these sources of power exist for them. For example, a newly qualified chemist might be more up-to-date in his knowledge of a particular process than his boss and thus be better placed to provide 'expert' guidance in this area, or because he is the one to do his bosses' 'legwork' may be able to pass on or usefully bias the information he acquires at grassroots level (Mechanic, 1962; Khan *et al.*, 1964; Pettigrew, 1972, 1973).

Moreover, these are additionally valuable sources of power, as they provide the junior manager with the means by which to gain and exploit other power sources, in particular '*position*' and '*resource*' power. 'Position' power stems from the formal rights and duties that are attached to any role which allows its incumbent the right of information, access to a variety of organizational networks (e.g., committee membership), and the right to organize. Such rights and duties provide the manager with a source of legitimacy, as subordinates feel they 'ought' to comply with his requests, given the taken-for-granted rules that support notions of hierarchy and position, irrespective of his individual qualities (Weber, 1947).[11] Moreover,

[11] This is not to suggest that charisma, or the ability of an individual to influence through the force of his personality, is a negligible power source. However, it does have the drawback of being non-transferable and, often, transitory. For example, the few personnel specialists that demonstrably have overcome the lack of authority in their roles and are highly regarded by the top management in their organizations, are often seen to have gained this position through their personal qualities and political skills alone. But their success is considered to reflect individual rather than departmental achievement and, as such, a reappraisal of personnel's contribution to organizational success becomes irrelevant. As

Cont. next page

once achieved, such a role is likely to provide a manager with access to resource power, in other words to that range of sanctions (such as the power to influence the size of salary increases, or promotion) available to reward support or compliance or to punish non-compliance or outright opposition (with-holding rewards, transfer into an unpopular job, and so on). (Conversely it should be noted, though, that if 'position' power is not ultimately underwritten by 'resource' power, if the organization does not provide such backing for the rights attached to a role, it becomes invalid as a power source. Whereas to some extent access to resource power is dependent on existing position power, position power is also dependent on resource power for its maintenance and development.)

To develop constructive relationships with existing power-holders, the manager not only needs the right of access, which he may obtain through his formal position, but he also needs sufficient political sensitivity to know how to relate the resources available to him to interests that are salient to those he wishes to influence, how to construct close relationships with those whose support will be valuable. This involves being aware of such factors as the degree of reciprocity involved in his contacts and the extent to which these relationships are uniplex or multiplex (Gluckman, 1956; Kapferer, 1969). What is meant by the latter is that, given that all interactions are composed of a number of transactions or exchange contacts (e.g., conversation, personal service, job assistance, and after-work social and sporting contact), multiplexity refers to relationships in which there is more than one exchange content, while a uniplex relationship has only one. Pettigrew (and others) argue that because multiplex relationships are generally considered closer and more enduring than those which are uniplex, the manager will be able to exert greater influence over those to whom he is multiplexly tied. These, of course, must be the 'right' individuals, as there is little return in cultivating those who lack, or are unlikely ever to obtain, power in the organization. Conversely, it is important for the aspirant individual to be aware of competitors for influence over existing power-holders, as what might in the present appear to be an advantageous alliance, in fact, may involve a growth in the influence of a potential rival.

Assuming that the manager has successfully identified and achieved access to the power-holders in his organization, his ability to develop close

---

Footnote 11 (*cont.*)

Herman puts it:

> Not many, but a few high personnel men have, by their personal qualities, made their way into the top management councils of their companies. If they remain, though, it is most often as tolerated guests rather than as recognized members of the family. *Their presence and their influence are based solely on their persuasive skills.* No operating charter, formal or informal, exists that entitles them to—or better still, imposes upon them—responsibility for participation in the organization's policy making (Herman, 1968, page 303).

(*My italics*)

relationships with them will to some extent depend on what Pettigrew has termed his 'assessed stature' (defined as 'the process of developing positive feelings in the perceptions of relevant others'). As he points out, this is related to what Goffman (1969) terms 'impression management', or the ability of the individual, through his knowledge of 'the facts of the situation', in interaction with others to create an image of himself consistent with their preferences and his own enlightened self-interest. Pettigrew argues that identifying the 'facts of the situation', in reality, is discovering what is *salient* to those individuals with whom the interaction takes place; in other words, what are their 'needs, expectations and reference group affiliations' (1976, page 201). If a manager wishes to generate high 'assessed stature' for himself and so appear credible to existing power-holders, it is argued he needs to anticipate what is salient to their interests, a process that is likely to be far easier if the existing relationships are multiplex rather than uniplex in character. Thus, for example, if the power-seeking individual wishes to generate support for a potential project among an influential group, he first builds up credibility with them by taking on activities perceived to be salient to their interests, and which, if successful, have highly tangible and visible outcomes. In this way, he can amass credits that may be cashed in when he needs support for a project whose salience is higher to him than to those whose support he is seeking. Because a manager's credibility is likely to vary over time and with different groups, if he wishes to use it effectively he must always be aware of 'how many credibility credits (he) has with (a) particular constituency (at any point in time) and to what power sources . . . they pertain, remembering always that what works in one constituency may not work in another' (Handy, 1976, page 129). Just as some groups or individuals respond to the use of certain power sources and not to others, so certain methods of influence are appropriate to one power source and not to another. For example, the manager needs to be aware that while expert power is best expressed through persuasion and not through force, so position power may be appropriately exercised through the institution of rules and procedures backed up by the judicious use of resource power, exercised through formal and informal processes of negotiation and exchange.

Clearly, there is a high level of overlap in these individual power bases. The greater, the scarcer, and the more sought after the level and nature of the individual's professional expertise, the easier it is for him to achieve political access and provide services salient to those whose support he seeks to obtain. The greater his political sensitivity, the easier it is for him to identify these saliences and enhance his credibility through appropriate use of his expertise. Thus, these factors tend to be mutually reinforcing.

Although the sources of power available at departmental and individual level have been discussed separately, up to this point, clearly they are interdependent. Thus, the more powerful a department/function becomes within an organization, the more likely it is to be able to attract to it individuals who not only have high levels of perceived expertise, but are presented with opportunities of obtaining access to the top power-holders because of the department's accepted importance to the organization as a whole. The more power a department has, the more resources it can obtain to facilitate its own growth, thus providing more promotion opportunities, or routes to 'position' power, for the individuals within it. Equally, the individuals who obtain power within the department are then responsible for making those 'strategic choices' that will largely determine their function's ability to control contingencies, itself a source of intra-organizational power (Child, 1972; Hickson *et al.* 1971).

Summary. This discussion would suggest that, in exercising the personnel function, a manager's power to implement the policies he believes are appropriate depends on a range of inter-related factors. These include:

1. The organization's dominant ideology.
2. The areas of contextual uncertainty it defines as being of crucial importance to resolve.   } Organizational factors
3. How it defines, measures, and evaluates success.
4. The manager's own level of expertise in the areas of activity he undertakes, whether specifically personnel management or not.
5. His right of access to those he needs to influence and from whom he requires information in order to design and implement policy.   } Individual factors
6. His ability to establish credibility with those individuals he seeks to influence and from whom he seeks support.
7. The resource power his position commands.

Before applying these ideas to a discussion of how the personnel function has actually been carried out in a range of organizations (chapter 3), it is necessary first to make a brief comment on the immediate context in which the exercise of functional and individual power may be observed.

The exercise of power in organizations

Most commentators are agreed that theoretically the exercise of power in organizations may be identified most clearly in the processes of decision-making[12] (Cyert and March, 1963; Etzioni, 1964; Pettigrew, 1973;

---

[12] It has been suggested, though, that, in practice, examining the exercise of power through the study of decision-making processes does involve several limiting assumptions. The first is that of the existence of observable conflict. This arises from the focus on decision-making itself, which naturally leads observers to concentrate on decisions of 'importance', or 'issues' in key areas, and the assumption here is that an 'issue' is likely to be controversial and that controversy and conflict go hand in hand. Thus, Polsby argues that identifying 'who prevails in decision-making' seems 'the best way to determine which individuals and groups have

Cont. next page

Lukes, 1974; Simon, 1976), especially in what has been termed 'strategic decision-making' (that which is involved in specifying goals and objectives and hence, major resource allocation in the organization) and 'administrative decision-making' (that which is concerned with structuring the organization's resources so as to create an optimum performance potential) (Ansoff, 1965). From an empirical research point of view, however, it is not always easy to gain access to these processes while they are ongoing, and often the best one can hope for is to gain the views of participants, after the decisions have been taken, about what happened and why. The problem here is that the resulting information may be as full of *post facto* rationalizations as it is of omissions.

Hence, of necessity, a broader approach needs to be taken. An examination of formal decision-making, such as can be practically undertaken, needs to be supplemented by an awareness that a 'policy' may be arrived at through decisions of an implicit nature, or by default, or being taken outside the formal identifiable channels, and that so-called 'decisions' may exist in name only due to resistance or inertia over their implementation. Rather than through examining processes of decision-making *per se*, the exercise of power may perhaps be more easily identified through an examination of implicit and explicit policy formulation and implementation, as perceived by their recipients as well as those more directly involved. It is this approach that guides the discussion in the next chapter.

Footnote 12 (*cont.*)

"more" power in social life, because direct conflict between actors presents a situation most closely approximating an experimental test of their capacities to affect outcomes' (1963, page 4). The problem with this assumption is that it does not allow for the identification of power in situations where conflict remains covert or latent. As Lukes comments:

> To put the matter sharply, A may exercise power over B by getting him to do what he does not want to do, but he also exercises power over him by influencing, shaping or determining his very wants. Indeed, is it not the supreme exercise of power to get another or others to have the desires you want them to have—that is, to secure their compliance by controlling their thoughts and desires? (1974, page 23).

This difficulty is related to a second limiting assumption implicit in the focus on observable decision-making. That is, it ignores the power exercised when an individual, or group, works behind the scenes to prevent potential issues, that in their resolution might be detrimental to their perceived interests, from ever reaching formal decision-making arenas. The problem then becomes that, although somewhere along the line decisions are made about a particular issue (e.g., that it should not be formally raised or discussed) that reflect the power of various participants, it is empirically difficult, if not impossible, to identify which individuals and what processes are involved in these covert activities. One method of doing so, still in the experimental stage, is being developed by Crenson (1971).

3. Power and authority in the personnel function: the reality

In the previous chapter it was argued that a function's intra-organizational power derives from its ability to create dependency, on the part of competing groups, for its services in controlling contingencies which the latter define as strategic to themselves and to the organization as a whole. Further, it was suggested that perceptions of what is 'strategic' and the capacity to gain control of such contingencies is determined by a network of 'normative expectations and understandings' (Whitley, 1975) or 'underlying rules' (Clegg, 1975) that arise out of the dominant ideology of the society in which the organizations exist. In western society, the prevailing managerial ideology tends to be a capitalistic utilitarianism, which, while it can be seen to exist in formal statements of organizational goals, at the operating level more realistically takes the form of the explicit and implicit success criteria, which provide the reference points for what is defined as legitimate policy formulation, implementation, and evaluation. As for the managers who actually exercise this power, their own authority may be seen to derive not only from their formal position or role in the organization, but from their managerial expertise, including both professional, interpersonal, and political skills, and from the material resources they can consequently control and utilize in such decision-making processes.

Having said this, what power do managers have to carry out the personnel function in accordance with their own policy preferences and definitions of the activity, whether as personnel specialists or line managers? The following discussion is based on a number of case studies[1]

[1] Much of these case study data were collected by Miss Margaret Exley, funded by a research grant from BP Ltd., to whom grateful thanks are extended.

of how the personnel function (both the activity and its institutionalized presence, the personnel department) actually operated in a range of organizations, varying in size and type of industry in the early 1970s. (Outline contextual details of the organizations involved are listed in Appendix I.) While space prohibits detailed analysis of each case study, material drawn from them will be used to illustrate the arguments presented below.

Personnel management and the non-specialist

From the case studies two major themes emerge. First, that while senior managements in the organizations involved were coming to a realization that 'something needed to be done' about personnel policies in their organizations, especially in the medium sized and small organizations, they lacked the ability to think through appropriate and internally consistent personnel management strategies. Second, that line managers, while recognizing that much of their work was a form of personnel management, tended to operate in this area in an *ad hoc* manner, without any clearly thought out and articulated framework to which to relate their activities. As a result, in company decision-making, the personnel management considerations involved in production, marketing, and finance decisions were not so much overruled (although this also occurred as will be discussed later), as went by default. In other words, non-specialists, while *formally* recognizing the importance of effectively utilizing human resources, lacking as they did the expertise to develop a systematic view of what this entailed in terms of personnel strategies and action, *in practice* tended to underestimate the importance of the human resource variable in decision-making on issues that were not explicitly 'personnel management'. While in theory they recognized that the effective use of manpower was of vital importance to their organizations, in practice the very pervasiveness of manpower management meant that, being taken for granted, it was neglected as a dimension to most problems under discussion and emerged as an issue worthy of concentrated consideration only if a specifically 'manpower' crisis threatened (cf., Crichton, 1968, page 328). Hence, although theoretically strategic to the organization, personnel management, even in its broadest sense, often was not perceived or treated as such.

These points are perhaps best illustrated by some examples.

The absence of systematically formulated personnel policies. In the larger, more sophisticated, companies (for example, Company A, a multi-national) policy documents existed which covered a broad range of personnel policy. These appeared to arise, as expected, both from the desire to facilitate uniform decision-making and implementation throughout these companies' geographically dispersed and diversified operations on such matters as salary administration, industrial relations procedures and practices, and management development, and, in those cases where a sophisticated capital intensive technology operated in competitive product and labour markets, from a realization that competitive edge rested largely on the efficient utilization of manpower.[2] The medium sized and smaller companies, however, tended either to have well-defined policies on certain issues (for example, on recruitment, conditions of employment, and collective bargaining arrangements) and none on areas less immediately pressing (for example, on management development), or to rely on a rudimentary policy on basic terms and conditions of employment backed by observance of legal obligations. Awareness of these inadequacies in policy formulation was not infrequent, but until specific incidents that could be directly costed and attributed to deficiencies in this area (such as strikes over parity claims due to a failure to set concrete guidelines on wage negotiations for different sites, or a pressing succession problem arising out of the absence of systematic and integrated management development and manpower planning), managements tended to shelve the issue. Justifications of inertia on this matter reiterate the old arguments about the difficulties of drawing up hard and fast rulings in a changing environment, for, as one company put it, 'while there is a need to define more precisely what our personnel policies should be, day-to-day practice will inevitably give rise to matters which call for re-interpretation and re-appraisal of policy to meet a dynamic situation'.

In fact, for large and small companies alike (if particularly evident in the smaller companies), what was clear from the case studies was the basically reactive nature of their policy formulation. Thus, areas that had not caused specific problems to date tended to be ignored, while the strongest stimulus to action was legislative. Companies B and C typically illustrate this

---

[2] Cf., for example, P. S. Linklater's (then Personnel Director of Shell UK Ltd.) comments on the relationship between capital intensity and commitment to systematic personnel management, including manpower planning:

> The competitive edge in the capital intensive industry really resides in the effective use of manpower, because even in chemicals (the other major capital intensive industry) there is a degree of technological stalemate. It is a remarkable contradiction that the manpower intensive industries (in the 1960s) were least interested in manpower savings; the emphasis of management in such an industry is related to the fact that a better profit than the competition was more readily secured by producing a better product, or to invest in new machinery to build an identical product more cheaply. The dynamic in the manpower intensive industries is in investment and technology and not in manpower. It is in the capital intensive industries that the dynamic is in manpower (1975, page 63).

For classic examples in the literature of large, capital intensive organizations, relative sophistication and willingness to innovate in areas of personnel policy and practice, see Flanders (1964) on Esso's early exercises in productivity bargaining, Paul and Robertson (1970) on ICI's programme of job enrichment, and Hill (1971) on Shell's experiment with OD. It should be borne in mind, though, that the implementation of these programmes often fell short of their conceptualization, or were not sustained. Cf., Klein's (1976) account of her experience at Esso (UK).

pattern. In Company B (a division of a large, chemical processing company), the major growth areas in terms of the employment of specialist staff in personnel management were in training and industrial relations, the respective increases in staff occurring at the time of the introduction of the Industrial Training Boards and the (now-repealed) Industrial Relations Act. In Company C, a medium sized engineering company, it was in the same period that their first specialist industrial relations manager and a management development advisor[3] were appointed, as, it will be seen, was the case in Company D.

Indeed, a good indicator of the extent to which any aspect of personnel policy has been consciously thought through and has real official backing is the quantity and quality of specialist staffing in that area and their reporting relationships, for the policies agreed at Board level tend to exist on paper alone unless resources are allocated and structures designed to facilitate their development and implementation. Too often in the smaller and medium sized companies, even where a specialist is appointed, the extent of the job involved (for example, to set up a management development programme from scratch, in a situation where even systematic job descriptions do not exist, let alone any proper system of management appraisal) requires more resources than senior management either realizes is necessary or is prepared to allocate. A case in point is what occurred in Company D, a medium sized food and animal feeds processing company. In 1970, following a period of acquisition and diversification, serious problems of integration threatening the firm's continued viability in an increasingly turbulent economic environment stimulated an examination of the company's deficiencies in internal organization and development. One outcome of this was to recognize that the 'human side' of the enterprise required attention and that 'something should be done'. This resulted in the following suggestions outlined in a policy memo on Personnel Organization (March 1970), formulated at Board level:

> There are considerable areas of personnel activity which must be developed to meet the needs of the Group. These are not being given sufficient attention because of the extreme pressures that are being applied elsewhere, particularly in the Industrial Relations field. These include Management Training and Development, formulation of comprehensive salary structures, involvement with an MBO programme, organizational and manpower planning, etc. In order to meet the criteria indicated above and maintain appropriate co-ordination coupled with direct involvement in subsidiary company affairs, it is proposed that three senior personnel officer positions should be established. These will be responsible to the Group Personnel Officer and provide a service within a defined (company product group) area . . . and the respective Senior Personnel Officers will be closely identified with the management of the company(ies) they serve.

---

[3] It was interesting that one year after his appointment in 1970, a very senior manager in the company was not aware that this role existed.

What these suggestions resulted in was merely the importation of one 'specialist' industrial relations manager, who was immediately thrown in to support industrial relations fire-fighting at plant level,[4] the promotion of an existing plant personnel officer to the role of group management development and training officer, and the upgrading of two plant personnel officers into senior personnel officers, responsible for integrating the activities of the plant personnel officers within the product group for which they were responsible. Additionally, a remaining plant personnel officer was appointed as the deputy to the new industrial relations manager, but as he remained located on the main production site of which he had been plant personnel officer, in practice he continued with much the same duties. Although the existing group personnel officer, who had previously been responsible for co-ordinating the activities of all the individual plant personnel officers, was now considered to have time to develop a management appraisal system and a new salary structure, in practice he became immersed in the support of the newly appointed senior personnel officers and co-ordination of their activities. Moreover, while the latter were supposed to analyse their product groups requirements for the services of the newly appointed specialists and thus provide support for them, they too were drawn into the day-to-day routine of plant level personnel administration, in the induction and support of their replacements. Hence, the specialists, lacking any real back-up in their diagnostic and planning activities, tended also to occupy themselves with the provision of day-to-day services, neglecting to develop the long-term policy framework necessary for real integration at group level. In other words, insufficient new resources were allocated to cope with the two major and inter-related personnel problems that the company faced: the integration of existing activities, and the development of group-wide policies and procedures in vital areas where at that time little systematic policy existed. The strategy of largely upgrading existing personnel staff into areas of responsibility for which they lacked both training and experience meant that, in reality, resources were increased only at the level of routine plant administration, as the so-called senior personnel officers and management development officer could not clearly differentiate their new roles from the old, while the recruitment of new staff (except for the industrial relations manager) was of junior officers at plant level.

An even more serious impediment to the formulation of company personnel policy occurs in the absence of any prior corporate plan.[5] In several of the companies studied, for example, Company F, a national

---

[4] Cf., Morris's (1972) comments about how quickly development roles can be undermined by the need to cope with associated routine activities.

[5] Cf., a recent IPM (1975) survey on manpower planning practices in British companies (N=308), in which over 75 per cent of the respondents, distributed through companies of all sizes and industries, agreed that 'Manpower planning suffers from non-existence of corporate plan" (Thakur, 1975, page 33). See also Foulkes (1977) on personnel's need to integrate policy-making with corporate strategy.

advertising agency and Company G, a batch engineering firm, either no corporate plan had ever existed or, following rapid changes in product demand, as in Company G, the corporate strategy was in the process of being totally revamped. In these circumstances, all personnel policy formulation, other than that required by legislation, tended either to be shelved or just not get off the ground due to the absence of fixed points of reference and a clear picture of overall company direction to which such policy might be related.[6] In Company F, for example, while most account directors (advertising's line managers) recognized the need for an explicit manpower plan, this failed to materialize. They could reach no agreement as to the future of the advertising industry as a whole and their organization in particular, some maintaining that advertising was entering a period of steady decline, others that it was about to take off into expansion. This confusion reinforced the Chairman's view that, in advertising, corporate strategy would take care of itself as long as the agency maintained the priority of learning techniques and discovering new methods to make advertising link more directly to the ultimate profitability of the client company. In practice, then, strategy was subsumed to function, and corporate planning and corporate objectives were seen mainly in terms of the immediate 'health' of certain accounts, alternative reactions to the strategies of client companies themselves, and the development of research knowledge in such areas as inter- and intra-media comparisons.

Finally, it is often overlooked that any type of long-term policy or strategy is vulnerable not only to the external pressures of environmental change—which might be anticipated—but to internal changes in managerial personnel, especially if it involves the top management of the company. Lisl Klein's (1976) account of the activities of the UK operations of Esso Petroleum Ltd., in the later 1960s, for example, shows clearly that when people retired, were promoted, or moved around, and newcomers took over certain strategic jobs, not only might existing plans have to be renegotiated with the new incumbents, who lacked the interest and commitment of their predecessors, but, in certain instances, the whole emphasis and direction of policy could change. In these circumstances, any innovatory or experimental developments were particularly prone to being halted, or even reversed, in mid stream. As Klein shows, while major shifts in policy could occur in all functional areas, personnel was uniquely susceptible to a 'swings and roundabouts' approach, as their resources, not being irreversibly committed in the form of technical hardware, were seen as being relatively flexible. Such practices inevitably pose threats for the establishment of coherent policy formulation and implementation.

[6] Similarly, there are frequent instances of how development activities, such as OD programmes, developed in conjunction with external consultants, have been abandoned prematurely due to simultaneous, but unco-ordinated, company re-organizations. A vivid example is provided by the fate of Esso's 'Michigan Project' which was effectively halted by its decision to re-organize the department, in which the experiment was continuing, on a business-line rather than a geographical basis. (See Klein, 1976, pages 164–169.)

Neglect of the human resource dimension in line management decision-making. Whilst this reflects the deficiencies in policy formulation and implementation discussed above, it also results from the ways in which problems are examined in companies. Usually, either reports are written or evidence taken from those considered to be the relevant functional specialists, and this may be discussed at committees of one sort or another. A problem here is that many issues that potentially have a direct bearing on human resource utilization are not considered from this perspective by the specialists concerned, while personnel specialists are not regarded as being legitimately involved. A case in point concerns product innovation. In many manufacturing organizations, specialists in design and marketing work together to produce a product that, it is hoped, will appeal to the consumer. While production specialists may be involved in the later stage of design to comment on the technical snags in production, it is unlikely that its implications for manpower development, training, and industrial relations will be considered until the designs have been finalized and production is about to commence. If, at this point, the implications of the design in industrial relations terms is pointed out, it is unlikely that serious modifications can be made, as the marketing strategy is probably well under way.[7] Yet, it is virtually unknown either for designers to think through the industrial relations (as opposed to technical) constraints that may influence the practical viability of a design, or for personnel specialists to be involved at this early stage. Although the theory of socio-technical systems has been around for years, managers are still inclined to concentrate more on the technical than the social, and show little interest or aptitude in building detailed models of their interaction. An apt illustration of this, attributed to Professor T. Lupton, is what has become known as 'The Story of the Pig'.

---

[7] Cf., the similar difficulties incurred by Lisl Klein as Esso's 'in-house' social scientist in the late 1960s, early 1970s of 'involving social science early enough, at the design stage of situations'. The following example that she quotes is typical of relevant expertise being sought too late:

> The opening of the new fuel-oil pipeline was scheduled for the autumn of 1969, and designs for the new building had to be approved at the beginning of the year. The engineer in charge of the construction was very willing to take advice. A major decision which had to be taken, for instance, concerned the site of the control room. One alternative was to build a new control centre at the entrance to the site, so that drivers would be given instructions as they drove out, and hand in documents as they drove in. This would also have the effect of geographically separating the control of loading from the physical operation of loading. The alternative was to extend the present loading and transport control room at the centre of the site. The engineer came to ask what the difference would be in terms of the social organization and attitudes of the drivers. Without doing some work with the drivers I could not tell him. I made a quick optimistic estimate that I could get an answer for him in three weeks, but there was no way of getting the investigation sanctioned quickly and he could not wait. Major consequences for work roles and group relations were, of course, implied in the decision, and the engineer realized this. He promised to leave as many design options as he could open for as long as possible, but this one decision had to be taken (1976, page 173).

In one of the slaughter houses of a meat products company, a dispute broke out between a group of slaughtermen and their foreman, during which the slaughtermen threatened to strike unless the foreman was immediately sent home. Management immediately agreed to their demand without an inquiry into the rights and wrongs of the parties' respective claims. The case eventually went to arbitration and, not surprisingly, the arbitrator asked why the foreman had been so summarily treated. The senior management replied 'Well, it's the question of the pig'. Apparently, in response to consumer demand for lean bacon, a particular type of pig had been bred for the company's farms which produced the maximum lean meat for the minimum cost. To produce an appropriate flow of pigs to meet levels and fluctuations in demand, a particular breeding cycle and rearing schedule was followed on the farms, so that the animals reached their optimum condition immediately before their planned dispatch to the slaughterhouse. Because calculation of production costs and consumer preference demanded immediate slaughter of the pigs after a fixed number of weeks' rearing, a complicated dispatch system had theoretically eliminated the desirability or necessity of large stock pens at the slaughterhouse, the animals moving, almost on a conveyor belt, from farm to slaughterhouse and ultimately to the customer. In theory, this system combined the production of the type of bacon demanded by the customer with an admirably tight control on costs of production and overheads. In practice, however, it gave the slaughtermen the whip hand. For, if they caused a bottle-neck in the throughput of pigs from slaughterhouse to customer, its repercussions were felt right back on the farm. Only a certain number of pigs could be kept alive in the stockyard and these would go rapidly past their peak and start putting on undesirable and expensive fat. The same could be said of the carefully scheduled pigs in delivery vans on the roads of England, who had no place to go to except back to the farms where they could only consume costly fodder, producing valueless fat, and utilizing accommodation required by their replacements. At the same time, constraints on stockholding, due to the perishability of the product, afforded management no alternative flexibility in maintaining market supply, if their slaughterhouse were out of operation, while the nature of the market demand and competition meant that sales lost in one period were unlikely to be recovered in another. A shut-down in the slaughterhouse thus meant irrecoverable losses in the product market, and hence direct implications for profitability. Thus, a product was designed that unintentionally delivered negotiating power straight into the hands of a strategically placed group of workers (Sayles, 1958). Yet, as the management sadly acknowledged, 'who would consider that industrial relations specialists should have been involved in the design of a pig and the successive scheduling arrangements?'

In theory, of course, it is recognized that such decisions—especially those of a long-term nature—should not be made without full consideration of all relevant information and points of view. Hence the attempts at project teams and various forms of matrix organization, not to mention the more conventional committee systems that exist in most organizations. In practice, though, even where such multi-functional gatherings take place, they tend to reflect the perspectives of those functions and managers who, at that time, hold power in the organization. Moreover, most participants in committee meetings are well acquainted with the practice that while each item on the agenda may be discussed at length, it is rarely the case, at the end of the meeting, to pause and systematically consider what implications the viewpoints expressed and decisions reached on each item have for each of the others, unless very obviously related.[8] For example, a typical weekly production meeting in a large batch production manufacturing industry chaired by a plant director or works manager might involve the consideration of such items as the state of the order book, patterns of product demand, the stockholding and supplies position, problems with delivery dates, the plant maintenance situation, costs against budget, and perhaps shortages of labour. It is likely the pattern of discussion will be for the functional specialist principally concerned with a particular area (e.g., the chief engineer with plant maintenance) to analyse the situation from his perspective and, following comments passed in reaction to his statements, a decision may be taken, or, if no immediate problem threatens, his comments may be noted and attention switched to the next item on the agenda. Either a topic will be treated in isolation, or, if related to other issues, it is likely to be those that are the focus of the meeting, in this case throughput in the plant and performance in the market. Thus, questions involving the utilization of human resources, for example, labour shortages, may be considered in terms of how they are adversely affecting production and, perhaps, how increases in overtime to attract labour might involve an increase in production costs, but it is unlikely the converse will take place. It is unlikely to be considered how variations in the materials used are upsetting bonus payments and leading to lower earnings and to labour

---

[8] Lisl Klein quotes a good example of management's ability to support mutually incompatible policies, owing to the fact that, being defined as functionally separate areas, the relationships between them were not considered. Writing of a re-organization of the marketing department in Esso in the late 1960s she describes the following confusion:

An evaluation of 'new deal' implementation had led management to the view that those aspects of the 'new deal' which had been controlled centrally had been successful, and those which had been left to local discretion, particularly in the setting and application of standards, had not. The conclusion drawn was that there should be closer control and tighter standards. Work-study consultants were being commissioned to devise centrally applied standards, and the industrial engineers were being instructed to devise ways of tightening control over such things as the quantities of product loaded and delivered. At the same time, the Operations Manager was enthusiastically supporting the Michigan project, with its expressed philosophy of devolving authority downwards and increasing the control which people at local level should have over their own affairs. Nobody could be persuaded to look at these two activities in relation to each other (1976, pages 153–154).

turnover, or how a different stockholding policy might provide a buffer in times of labour shortage. At best, the human relations dimension might be considered in terms of its effect on production and costs, but it is unlikely that decisions taken about the design, costing, and batch size of the product will be considered in relation to the effects they might have on the human resources involved. Human resources, it might be argued, are just that, existing to facilitate performance in the market place, not *vice versa* (according to the dominant capitalist ideology), so it is not surprising that the direction of influence is seen from the one perspective. Unfortunately, in the long term, this tendency to ignore the fact that the influence works both ways can undermine product market objectives.

An example of this has been described in some earlier work (Legge, 1970). In a medium sized company manufacturing childrens' clothes in the late 1960s, in response to consumer demand and in an attempt to maintain market share in the face of intensifying competition, the management decided to develop an increasingly wide range of small batch 'fashion' garments and to abandon their previous concentration on long-run 'bread and butter' lines where margins were small, competition from imports intense, and opportunities for growth limited. Thus, whereas prior to the change in policy, management would reckon to carry through to the next season a minimum of 50 per cent of the styles, 30 per cent with minor modifications, while only 20 per cent would be new styles, after the change in market policy, the position was reversed, with 50 per cent of the styles being entirely new, 25 per cent being modifications of the existing range, and only 25 per cent of the styles being carried through from the previous season. At this stage, line management's only awareness of the potential repercussions of their marketing and production strategies was that more training might be required at the beginning of each season and that efforts at recruitment of machinists, in a tightening labour market, should be intensified to meet an anticipated upsurge in orders. At the meetings called to discuss the implications of this change in policy at factory level, not only were the product market decisions presented as a *fait accompli*, but the personnel manager's role was clearly seen as one of offering suggestions about how to accommodate them *via* amendments to recruitment strategies and extensions in training facilities, not of pointing out the possible repercussions on the whole production system of decisions already made without his advice.

What actually happened when this policy was implemented was as follows. The short production runs and frequent changes to new garments[9] undermined the existing highly geared incentive payment system as the machinists found it difficult to reach standard performance before changing on to a new production run, and thus spent increasing proportions of time

[9] Note that a job change for a machinist was likely to involve (a) machine change (b) operation change (c) material change, and as such involved potential learning difficulties in three areas.

on the low fall-back rate[10] that operated if standard performance was not reached. Earnings dropped and, given the competitive nature of the local labour market at that time, labour turnover increased, particularly among those machinists who sought high earnings for high effort, and who, under the previous production policy, had been amongst the highest performers.

The effect of this labour turnover was exacerbated due to the sectional ized flow production method employed, as gaps in the flow line left by departing members of the work team had to be covered to keep production running without major hold-ups and bottle-necks. This meant more job changing for the remaining machinists, lower performance, consequently lower earnings, and further absenteeism and turnover as they sought and left for other jobs. Given the short production runs, it was also a frequent occurrence that by the time a replacement had been recruited and trained to do the job of a leaver and assigned to a work team, that team could be about to start new work, necessitating a further period of training for the recruit on the low fall-back rate. This, added to the usual problems of induction, led to a high turnover of recruits. The company was therefore confronted with a situation in which they were experiencing difficulty in meeting delivery dates and, rather than expanding production as planned, they were barely able to keep enough labour to operate at pre-change levels of production. This had arisen through management's inability to see that the changes in market strategy that they proposed were likely to have an immediate impact on the existing wage payment system, which unless redesigned to lessen the effect of these changes on earnings levels, would result in self-perpetuating labour turnover, jeopardizing their proposed initiative on recruitment and training, and ultimately the marketing strategy itself.

Further, when awareness of these problems started to filter back up to senior management, their response was not to seek the underlying cause, but to involve themselves in emergency stop-gap measures to treat the symptoms. Work was contracted out and the personnel manager urged to step up recruitment. Given the tightness of the labour market, this led to increased recruitment of immigrants and part-timers, involving further problems of training and work scheduling. At no time was any attempt made to systematically analyse why market strategy and production policy were adversely affecting the utilization of the workforce: the management's perspective was entirely that problems with human resources (due to 'the tight labour market beyond our control', or 'lack of school leavers') were undermining their marketing and production strategies.

Numerous examples of this perspective among senior management, particularly of small and medium sized companies, could be illustrated from available case-study material. The reader is referred, for example, to

[10] Both line and personnel management freely admitted that the fall-back rate was kept deliberately low, in order to 'encourage' machinists to learn quickly in order 'to get on to piecework'.

the CIR series of reports,[11] that document similar cases of management's neglect to consider the repercussions of marketing and production decisions upon their labour force. As the CIR (Report No. 5) wrote of BSR Ltd., 'the success of the company's products in the markets of the world meant that management had to concentrate, to the virtual exclusion of all else, on increasing output. Success had meant rapid growth in the number of people employed, yet the management team had remained small. The problems arising from the needs and aspirations of a large number of people had been largely shelved under the pressure of the more immediate need to meet production targets' (page 12, para 34). Elsewhere (CIR Report No. 34), the Commission was forced to conclude (in reference to a sample of 23 companies 'chosen so as to illustrate a variety of different circumstances, relating particularly to each company's size and complexity of organization and the industry in which it operates') that 'a dominant impression gained from many companies was that industrial relations did not receive the attention they need along with commercial and operational matters' (page 5, para 19).

Yet, why is this so when senior line managers formally admit the importance of effectively utilizing human resources if organizational objectives are to be achieved? The official recognition and practical neglect of the human resource dimension in much policy formulation and implementation, at least until very recently, would appear to stem from the value system that is embodied in the success criteria employed to evaluate organizational and managerial performance, and which, as already argued, is the ultimate source of managerial power. In a capitalist society in which industrial and commercial organizations are ultimately answerable to their shareholders, the values that are likely to take priority are financial and these are likely to be reflected in the measures of organizational performance. Growth of assets, of rate of return on capital invested, of margins of profitability, of market share, and of output are all quantifiable in tangible monetary terms and in practice are likely to take priority over such intangibles as 'a high level of employee morale' unless this too can be quantified and its relationship to organizational success similarly measured.[12] From the prevailing view of what constitutes organizational

[11] See for example, 'BSR Ltd.' (Report No. 5); 'Armstrong Patents Company Ltd.' (Report No. 13); 'Clayton Dewandre Company Ltd.' (Report No. 15).

[12] Klein made a similar point strongly in a presentation to the Esso Board (in 1969) on the problems of getting social science knowledge (often described as the 'technology of personnel management') used as an input to organizational decision-making:

Every system or gadget that is introduced brings with it social and organizational consequences, whether you like it or not, and it should be completely axiomatic that people take steps to predict these and to cope with them. It is not difficult to persuade middle managers of the sense of this because they know it. But they won't do it until you hold them accountable in this way. When some bright spark comes to you with his pet project, ending up with a flourish that it will save 30 per cent of manpower and the

Cont. next page

success derives managerial objectives, which may not only define a manager's role through laying down a formal set of job requirements in the light of the organizational success criteria, but provide a framework upon which his evaluation may be based. And the greater the similarity of the terms in which organizational, functional (or departmental), and managerial success are expressed and measured, the more directly a management function can demonstrate its positive contribution to organizational performance. Thus, for example, a clear relationship might be demonstrated between an organization's rate of growth (an indicator of organizational success) and the achievement of individual sales targets (a sales manager's success criterion). Or, between profitability, growth in the value of production (a functional achievement), and an individual manager's success in achieving the greater quantity and quality of output on a given assembly line.

The problem of measuring the value of effectively utilizing human resources is that, because almost all managerial activity involves the use of this resource, its contribution to the final outputs, by which performance at all levels is measured, is difficult to disentangle from the other variables (such as the capital equipment) involved. Hence, it is often taken as given. This attitude of treating human resources as a 'black box' is also a result of management's ignorance and scepticism of, or confusion about, theoretically and empirically grounded models of human behaviour.[13] In their absence, those that managers cling to, such as 'It's well known that human nature doesn't change' or 'Most workers are only interested in the pay', and other shibboleths, tend to treat this resource as one whose few simple properties are known to present problems, which may be accepted as ultimately intractable due to its unchanging nature.[14]

[13] Cf., a story quoted by Klein, again during her time with Esso.

> ''You see', one director explained, 'the Chairman and I went to the States one time. He went to Harvard and I went to MIT. He came back saying that you mustn't have wide spans of control, and I came back saying that you mustn't have long lines of command. So we looked at each other and said "to hell with it", and got on with our jobs' (1976, page 28).

Note that both managers appear to have fallen foul of an inadequate prescriptive approach, similar to that criticized in chapter 1 of the present book.

[14] However, there is some ambiguity here. Although many managers tend to treat their workforce as a given, when they do think of using some social science input say, from external consultants, there often appears a preference for psychological rather than sociological models in problem analysis and solution. My own continuing research in the
Cont. next page

Footnote 12 (cont.)

> discounted cash flow is—you should be asking him 'What are the changes in skills, in demands, in roles and relationships and in organization that the remaining 70 per cent will be faced with, and what are you doing about that? And what mistakes will the remaining 70 per cent make as a result of the changes and how does that affect your DCF calculation?' Do that a few times and this company will be utilizing social science very quickly' (1976, page 186).

Further, where attempts are made to isolate its contribution (for example, in the measurement of individual output levels of different operators, for incentive payment purposes), the tendency is to focus on those contributions alone that are amenable to direct measurement and to ignore those that are not. Moreover, the fact that in terms of market value, short-term profits frequently take precedence over long-term prospects of growth, encourages a definition of 'effectiveness' in utilizing human resources that may, in the long term, act to the contrary. For example, the policy of making labour redundant in response to downturns in the economy may, in the short term, produce a saving on labour costs, but in the medium term reduce efficiency in manpower deployment on the remaining production (Martin and Fryer, 1973) and, in the long term, by damaging the firm's reputation in its local labour market, undermine its ability to recruit the right quality and quantity of labour when required. This is quite apart from the hypothesized relationship (for example, in shipbuilding) between periodic redundancies and short-time, in response to market demand, and subsequent suspicion of, and resistance to, capital investment, whether ultimately it will lead to a reduction in the labour force or not. Similarly, the practice of refusing to mediate threats of strike action when market demand is slack, in order to economize on short-term labour costs and, by reducing stock levels, on overheads (a practice well known in the British motor industry in the 1960s) (Turner *et al.*, 1967) may in the long term institutionalize a union response of resorting to strike action as a first, rather than last, counter in the bargaining process, with costly losses of production and delays in delivery when demand is buoyant. Notable too is line management's practice of using reward systems to facilitate the achievement of this month's production targets (e.g., through the over-generous use of overtime and the condoning of loose incentive times, in order to attract and retain labour and minimize the likelihood of hold-ups through disputes or labour shortages), without thinking through the long-term implications on labour costs of such short-term manipulations (e.g., institutionalized overtime, differentials disputes, overmanning combined with resistance to flexibility) (Gowler, 1969).

The combination, on the part of most line managers, on the one hand of taking its human resources for granted and on the other of defining effectiveness largely in terms of short-term financial results, in practice has

---

diminished the value placed on the contribution of good human resource management to organizational success *in its own right*. In these circumstances, while in theory good personnel management remains 'very close to the heart of the business', in practice it has either been taken for granted or, until a crisis threatens, remains a low priority for investment of the vital resources of time and systematic consideration by senior management. Thus, in terms of Hickson *et al.*'s argument, management in general tend not to perceive the human resource variable as presenting uncertainties whose resolution is vital to organization success, and in this they are supported by the value systems that dominate all cost-conscious organizations. Whether this situation is changing or not, and why, will be considered in the next chapter.

As an interest in, and skills in, dealing with the human resource dimension to organizational problems has appeared questionable as a source of power in organizations, where has this left the personnel specialist? To answer this we now turn to consider what power personnel specialists exercise in organizations.

Personnel management and the specialist

First, how are personnel specialists (i.e., those employed on general as well as specialist managerial tasks in the personnel department) regarded by line and other managers? What sort of role are they seen to play in the management of a company? The following quotations drawn from managers at plant level in the case study companies are representative of the type of response we elicited (for outline contextual details of the companies involved, see Appendix I):

> The trouble with the Personnel Department here is that they try to introduce gimmicky new theories through general management channels. They should stick to welfare—that's what personnel's job is—looking after routine welfare matters. (Assistant Works Manager (Engineering), Company A.)
> The Personnel Department is important in that both the Industrial Relations Officer and the Personnel Superintendent are anchor men who provide continuity of experience and interpretation of company policy. (Assistant Works Manager (Operations), Company A.)
> The Industrial Relations Officer does a great job offering policy advice, interpretations and guidelines for us. But I don't know what the Personnel Superintendent does to warrant his position. He just seems to act as a postillion between X and London on intra-company postings. (Works Manager, Company A.)
> The main job of the Personnel Department is to keep management informed of personnel policies both here and at other group chemical locations. (An Operations Manager, Company B.)
> The statistics they give us do not provide the information we need. (An Operations Manager, Company B.)
> OD's doing a good job, I think, but a lot of my colleagues are worried that it's almost impossible to measure its real impact as there are so many variables to be considered in the effectiveness equation. (An Operations Manager, Company B.)
> Personnel is not emotionally profit-oriented. I suppose this isn't really surprising

as a lot of their work is more an act of faith than anything. But I do sometimes think that they'd be more effective if they could justify their work in a more cost-conscious way. (An Operations Manager, Company B.)

The Personnel Department have little understanding of line management's problems. (Work Study Manager, Company C.)

In this company the Personnel Department should be mainly concerned with career development—providing an overview when two departments are in opposition. But it's not used in this way mainly because it doesn't have enough power and status within the company to act as a lever. So people don't use it and it tends to get ignored, except on small administrative details. (Head of Representatives, Company F.)

We're all personnel managers here. We have to be, as the only resources we've got is people. (Director, Company F.)

I have little time for Personnel. When recruiting they have little idea of what these men are supposed to do. We have to closely recheck them. Personnel officers would become more effective if they spent some time on the shop floor. Their approach is too academic. (Shift Supervisor, Company H.)

'Personnel should largely comprise an information and advisory function for line management. There is little point in worrying too much about motivation, the hourly paid do what they are told anyway. The problem is to chop out the dead wood and tidy up the recruitment. (Assistant Works Manager, Company H.)

In this industry (Entertainments), which is so decentralized—and has to be, for decisions must be made on the spot—we've really no need for a personnel department at all. I'm my own personnel manager to all intents and purposes, and have very little contact with our personnel department. (Unit Manager, Company I.)

The personnel department here is, as it should be, a service to the line. For example, if we want more labour they get it, train it, and arrange for it to be paid. They provide information for negotiations too, but I do the real negotiating. (General Works Manager, Company J.)

These comments were drawn largely from middle and senior plant/factory management about their impressions of the personnel departments with which they had varying degrees of contact. These mainly comprised the departments at plant level, but as personnel management at Group Head Office and divisional level impacted on plant line management through such activities as OD, manpower planning and management development, their awareness of these activities was also a factor in their impressions. However, as it was the plant's personnel departments which were largely responsible for transmitting and operationalizing company wide policies in the plant, line management often tended to equate the two and, in generalizing about the function throughout the company, drew mainly on their own experience of the personnel specialists in their own plant.

It is interesting that these comments are echoed by those of a group of American managers,[15] drawn from 'one large industrial organization',

[15] The managers interviewed numbered 147, and were drawn from corporate, divisional, and plant levels. They included all members of the corporate policy committee, most functional department heads, all general managers, selected managers of a variety of functional departments, many plant managers and their immediate subordinates—quite apart from members of the personnel department from all levels in the organization. (Ritzer and Trice, 1969, pages 64–65).

(see Ritzer and Trice (1969)). They saw their personnel departments as

1. Reacting to, rather than anticipating problems.
2. Passive—not an initiator nor a stimulator.
3. Defending the *status quo* rather than being creative and attempting to exercise leadership.
4. Carrying out management decisions, but not helping to shape management thinking.
5. Not standing up to be counted.
6. Not a risk-taker.
7. Not business-oriented.
8. Not involved in the personnel aspects of business decisions.
9. Having very little influence with management.
10. Operating in a vacuum (1969, page 65).

Moreover, Foulkes (1975, 1977) records virtually identical perceptions of their personnel departments on the part of the American line managers from a range of organizations, whom he interviewed and taught.

Concentrating on the comments of the British managers (although as will be indicated, where appropriate, to some extent they reflect each manager's own role within a particular company context), two major themes emerge common to most companies, *irrespective of size, operating processes, or industry*. They may be stated as follows:

1. Line management tend to have a confused, hazy, and/or stereotyped perception of the potential nature and scope of a personnel department's activities.
2. Middle and junior line management in particular tend to consider that personnel departments are 'out of touch' with the kind of problems and constraints which face them.

Interestingly enough, it was found in the case study companies, and in the American example (Ritzer and Trice, 1969, pages 72–75), that the personnel department's own perceptions of what they were actually able to do (as opposed to what they felt they should be doing) did not substantially contradict line management's rather dismissive view of them.[16] To develop this suggestion, these two themes are discussed in more detail.

Line management's confused and stereotyped perception of the activities of the personnel department.   Most line managers interviewed, irrespective of company, were quite clear on one issue, that an organization's personnel department existed to provide a service to the line, and that the line had the right to decide what this service should be. However, when encouraged to state what kind of service ideally they would wish to have provided, many of the managers particularly, but not exclusively, in the small and

---

[16] In contrast, in an earlier study, French and Henning (1966) found that personnel managers tended to perceive themselves as having more power than either their superiors, or colleagues in other functions perceived them to have.

medium sized companies, were at a loss to suggest anything other than the provision of routine services. (Similarly Ritzer and Trice, (1969, page 72) noted that top management's criticisms of corporate and divisional personnel managers were general rather than specific). In those companies which possessed systematically formulated company-wide personnel policies and procedures (notably the large, capital intensive, process technology companies such as Companies A, B and H), most senior line managers agreed that specialists' advice was useful in interpreting Head Office policy *vis à vis* industrial relations and terms and conditions of employment, and while all managers irrespective of company, conceded that personnel had a role in 'welfare', beyond this no very clear conception (and in most cases, no conception at all) existed of how personnel should develop its longer term activities, such as OD, management development, and manpower planning at plant level. In so far as there was a view at all, these were seen to be the activities of personnel 'research' departments, who, encapsulated in Head Office, were considered to devise schemes of dubious practical relevance to the operating manager, but which at the same time sought to involve him in tedious data collection exercises. The more informed managers tended to feel that on principle such activities as OD and management development 'must be a good thing', but were unable to suggest, other than in the most general way, what were the anticipated benefits of these activities, and whether they would outweigh the costs of implementation.[17]

Hence, at one level line managers appeared content to accept a type of personnel department that was fixed at an embryonic stage of development, that is, one that concentrated on providing the routine services or 'necessary chores' as Drucker put it, of personnel administration. At first sight, their view of what personnel 'should' be reflected that range of activities that they actually experienced as the work of the personnel department on a day-by-day basis. Superficially, and especially among junior and middle line management, their criticisms related much more to the inadequacies of *how* this service was carried out than to its scope. Thus, while in the majority of companies, first line management criticized personnel's performance in the selection of the right quantity and quality of recruits at the right time, no one suggested that an absence of systematic manpower planning might have contributed to an inadequate performance. But, at another level, their frequent criticisms that personnel specialists were 'out of touch' with the operating areas of the company, that they did not provide relevant statistics (or any statistics at all), etc., suggest an awareness of the *results* of inadequate diagnostic, planning, and developmental activities, even if it was not matched by an articulated recognition of where the *cause* lay. Thus, overt expressions of satisfaction with the

[17] Cf., the recent IPM survey that found similar confusions among personnel specialists in 16 British companies 'selected on the basis of their known interest and activity in the training and development field' (Thakur, 1974).

existing narrow scope of personnel administration, as they experienced it, sit uneasily with criticisms of content that implicitly question the scope of these services.

This confusion reflects a point made earlier. Just as line managers tend to take their human resources for granted, so too do they take for granted the personnel department they inherit. It is not an area of priority for evaluation and redesign. In this context, it is interesting that in the case-studies, particularly at plant level, and in the small and medium sized labour intensive technology companies, we found that personnel departments are still something of the backwater that they were traditionally represented to be. To a far greater extent than at the equivalent level of line management, we found that personnel managers tended to have remained stuck in the same department and in the same plant, while managers in other functions either moved between plants, or up or out of the company at a far greater rate.[18] This, for example, would be true of the situation in Companies A, C, D, E, F, I and J. The lack of mobility here tends both to reflect and exacerbate the situation in which personnel departments are taken for granted as the providers of traditionally defined services. Personnel managers whose major expertise is historical knowledge of a plant, superior to that of its more mobile line managers, are likely to have their chances of mobility reduced precisely because they are seen to provide the line with a continuity of experience and interpretation of company policy as it relates to that plant. This gives rise to fewer openings for younger, perhaps more professionally trained managers. In addition, the image of this type of department, where expertise and experience are equated, is likely to be unattractive to such managers anyway.

In these circumstances, such a personnel department has little stimulus (other than legislative) to change. Internally, it is likely to accept line management's traditional, unreflective definition of its role. This can result in the sort of situation recently described by Clive Jenkins who, in discus-

---

[18] Cf., similar recent evidence, drawn from a survey conducted in the British engineering industry, about the lack of mobility among training officers (EITB, 1974). In an editorial comment on this report in the journal *Personnel Management* (**6**, 2, February 1974), it was stated that

> With the exception of a spell in the forces, most training officers have had no experience outside their present firm. Moreover the majority of them are located in small departments which occupy in the main a very low place in the firm's organization structure. The head of the training department generally reports to a personnel specialist who—sad to tell—is himself only at middle management.
> The gloomy story unfolds with details not so much of his responsibilities but of those denied him, for (he) is seldom concerned with management training and development, organizational review and analysis, manpower planning or costing and budgeting. His job description of necessity tallies with the status of the department, the day to day activities which most concern him being the establishment of training procedures and the organization and administration of supervisor, operator and craft training.

For a similar view, see also Prentice (1975).

sing personnel managers' lack of power to authorize settlements in negotiations,[19] wrote,

> A vicious circle has been created whereby the brighter managers steer clear of
> the personnel function because of its lack of status, and in consequence the
> personnel function remains in low regard because of its relative lack of
> talent . . . (1973, page 35).

When, as was the situation in the early 1970s, salaries for personnel
managers trailed those of other managerial groups (AIC Management
Consultants, 'Survey of Executive Salaries and Fringe Benefits', 1970,
1971, 1972), this situation was further exacerbated. Moreover, this comment has extremely serious implications for the power of personnel specialist, when it is remembered that expertise is generally considered one of
the chief bases of managerial power. Again, it is interesting that Ritzer and
Trice's American managers made similar comments about the personnel
department's 'lack of professionalism' (1969, page 66) and the absence of
'necessary expertise' (page 69).

Although line management's acceptance of a personnel department
limited in scope and ambition may have advantages for the personnel
manager who wants an undemanding and safe job, the other side of the
coin is the reinforcement it provides to their neglect of the personnel
management perspective on 'non-personnel' problems, as discussed
earlier. The following is a typical pattern that emerges, but perhaps most
notably in those labour intensive companies, where the demands of
competitive product and labour markets, combined with highly inter-
dependent work-flow processes, stimulate *ad hoc* decision-making and
management. Line management, although nominally satisfied with the
service it receives from the personnel department, having defined its scope
narrowly, excludes the department from decision-making in areas such as
production scheduling, stockholding, etc. Neglect of the personnel dimension at this level can give rise to unequivocally personnel problems (such as
in the areas of recruitment and training) that, falling within the scope of
even the most narrowly traditional department, have to be coped with,
often without full knowledge of their causes, yet with extreme urgency.
Crisis management results. This may involve stop-gap measures, creating
unfortunate precedents for future bargaining, while offering only a partial
or inadequate solution to the problems involved. Line management then
gains an unfavourable impression of the department's ability to handle
even those problems that come within its scope, and has reservations about
any extension of its area of responsibility (see Fig. 3.1).

In other words, defining the role of a personnel department in narrow
traditional terms is likely to be self-perpetuating, as its exclusion from

---

[19] Cf., Ritzer and Trice's reporting of the views of the 'top level personnel management', in
the case study they presented, that 'top management had actively kept personnel out of
areas such as negotiations' (1969, page 73).

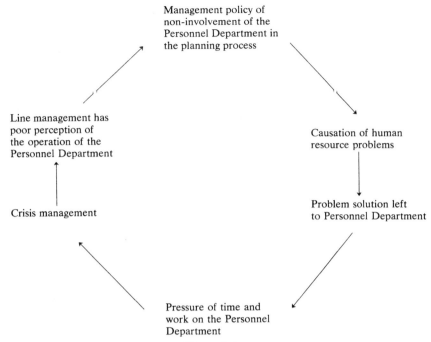

Figure 3.1.

planning and developmental activities is likely to render it even less effective in dealing with those 'personnel' problems recognized as its responsibility, confirming line management in their view that personnel's responsibilities should be of the routine kind. This in turn inhibits the recruitment of talent to such a personnel department, encourages turnover amongst those with either the talent or professional training to aspire towards a more demanding role for the department, and effectively de-skills those that remain.

Further, while it is difficult to encourage the most professional personnel managers to take over such a department, even the provision of training and development for its existing staff would not necessarily break the vicious circle. For, if this occurred, and the department tried to break out of its traditional 'canteens, hire, and fire' image and involve itself in sophisticated human resource management and policy-making decisions, the 'personnel specialists' involved would probably lack the credibility and bargaining power to gain the information and support from other departments (still seeing them in their old image) necessary for them to assume new areas and modes of operation.[20] Without the use of relevant in-

---

[20] Indeed, Herman quotes data from an (American) Industrial Relations Institute Survey, that a quarter of the personnel specialists questioned complained that they did not get advance information of company plans and actions affecting their own function (see Herman, 1968, page 26).

formation and without political support within the organization for the personnel department to assume a more adventurous role, such new activities as it undertakes, starved of resources, are likely to be unsuccessful. This in turn confirms the old stereotype and the view that it is not worth co-operating with the personnel department, as it has demonstrated that it is not competent to operate in these areas anyway. Thus, a vicious circle of information denial, lack of support, and credibility is set up which, by opposition, only serves to illustrate the mutually reinforcing relationships between power, resources, expertise, and credibility.

Line management's perception that personnel departments are 'out of touch' with their problems.   A typical example of this criticism is that related by a middle level line manager in Company E, a medium sized but capital intensive pharmaceutical company. Confronted by the problems of running a process production, highly interdependent technology but engaged on relatively small batch production, he perceived a need for some manning flexibility that was denied him by his (then) tight labour market environment, combined with head office directives about efficient labour utilization and control of labour costs. In his eyes, personnel had no understanding of the difficulties in which these conflicting demands placed him:

> Personnel don't seem to realize just how undermanned we are since their last productivity agreement. In cases of sickness and holiday absence, we are supposed to be able to draw on a labour pool for replacements. But these are still newcomers who are in the pool supposedly to get experience of a range of plants and for training, or they are the least able operators that no plant wants and who shouldn't have been taken on in the first place. Either way they are not much use except for menial jobs. Added to this, personnel are now saying that we've got to restrict the use of overtime, and this will mean that we can't use to the full those experienced men that we do have. As a result expensive plant will just not be used efficiently. Personnel just don't seem to understand this.

To many line managers, personnel's 'being out of touch' often reflects their perception that a general policy has been designed, perhaps based on insufficient or poor analysis by those involved, that pays too little attention to their own local difficulties and peculiarities. Clearly, the emphasis of line management's criticism varied depending on the position and organizational context of the manager involved. For example, in the larger and more sophisticated companies, where head office had developed standardized and comprehensive personnel policies and procedures to be operated on a company-wide basis, criticism tended to concentrate on problems resulting from the generality of their application, rather than on the quality of analysis on which the policy was based. But, while junior and middle management, who had to cope with the day-to-day problems of matching general, often constraining, guidelines to individual operating conditions, tended to be most critical of the difficulties this caused, senior line management were more prepared to recognize that on certain occasions, such as in negotiating situations, standardized policies could prove supportive just as much as frustrating. In contrast, in the medium sized and smaller, often labour intensive, organizations, the accusation that personnel specialists were 'out of touch' on the one hand reflected senior line management's exclusion of personnel from all but the most marginal of advisory roles in major decision-making, on the grounds of their low levels of expertise, and on the other, junior and middle managements' conviction that they were and had to be the real plant personnel managers, exercising the personnel function in its broadest sense. As one engineering supervisor put it, 'Personnel do the job theoretically, but we do it practically'. Yet, such criticisms go hand in hand with line's general reluctance, as discussed earlier, to allow personnel specialists into areas of decision-making and analysis that are not overtly 'personnel', and their lack of ideas about how personnel specialists may be used in a more analytical and developmental capacity than at present. Indeed, their own emphasis on the day-to-day problems of manning and industrial relations, often symptoms of more fundamental problems, inevitably reinforces personnel's existing preoccupation with crisis management and fire-fighting activities. While the cry of 'personnel is out of touch' may reflect a dissatisfaction with the quality of analysis and decision-making in this area, its immediate effect is again to maintain the existing situation by demanding speedy, and hence inevitably, short-term solutions in response to their problems. For instance, in the example discussed above, personnel responded to line's persistent complaints about undermanning, not by analyses of working patterns within the plant, prior to any decision-making about the best course of action, but by simply increasing the size of the labour pool, justifying this action on the grounds that it would provide some slack to facilitate the training programme. The only result of this was line management complaining that the quality of the labour in the pool was worse than ever, and that personnel 'had not and did not seem able to get to grips with the real problem'.

What do these perceptions of their personnel department by line management indicate about the position of personnel specialists in many organizations? It may be argued that it suggests that not only have they lacked the authority to gain acceptance of the theorists' conception of what a specialist department should be and do, but that, because of this, they have been unable to satisfy fully management's more mundane requirements of them. This, it may be argued, further diminishes such authority as they possess, and thus gives rise to an apparently self-perpetuating situation.

Yet, to go back to the question raised in the previous chapter, why is it that personnel specialists lack authority in the first place? To answer this, it is now necessary to return to the question of organizational success criteria. For, as was argued earlier, quite apart from the authority an *individual* manager can gain through his own professional, interpersonal, and political skills, any managerial *function's* authority within an organization ultimately rests on the extent to which its activities are perceived by existing power-holders to be vital to the achievement of those indicators or success criteria accepted to represent the achievement of organizational goals or ends.

Personnel management and organizational success criteria

In the previous chapter, it was suggested that not only is it impossible to arrive at a single definition of what is meant by the personnel function, but that this confusion is reflected in the specialist department's dilemma as to whether they should emphasize the 'personnel' or the 'management' side of their work, and in their lack of a clear understanding of what the aims and scope of their work should be, quite apart from sorting out priorities according to the specific needs of the situation. As Herman has commented, 'the real poverty of the personnel field stems from the failure of personnel men to determine the purpose of their function' (1968, page 5). This is not surprising when, as discussed earlier, both the boundary between the personnel department and the personnel function is confused, as is that between the personnel function and other management activities. In the face of such ambiguities, as Drucker points out, it is only too easy for personnel's confusion about what it should be doing to be exacerbated, giving rise to their dysfunctional collection of a 'hodge-podge' of unrelated activities.

Such observations indicate the difficulty of relating the personnel function (and its specialist roles) to organizational success criteria (or, in Hickson *et al.*'s terms, make visible its 'centrality'), since there is a real problem in determining how 'personnel' does or should contribute to ultimate aims and objectives. Thus, there is another vicious circle here. Personnel has difficulty in defining what it should be doing because of the difficulty of relating potential 'personnel' activities directly to the achievement of organizational ends, yet this lack of definition, by encouraging the undirected collection of a 'hodge-podge' of miscellaneous activities, further confuses the question of its contribution to organizational success.

Some empirical evidence underlines this dilemma. McFarland, in a survey sponsored by the American Management Association, found that while personnel specialists occasionally state the objectives of their department in the same broad terms as the textbooks, for example, as being

> The administration and co-ordination of human resources of the company in keeping with the ultimate goals of the company in providing a service to society as well as bringing a fair financial return to the stockholders (Chemical company) (1967, page 16).

in practice, they generally abandon the attempt to define their objectives in terms of organizational ends, and treat the means to these ends (i.e., personnel programmes, particularly those concerning manpower acquisition and development) as ends in themselves. Indeed, the survey results would suggest that although individual personnel specialists believe that personnel departments should be deeply involved in corporate matters such as organizational planning and company policy *vis à vis* productivity and efficiency, in practice the majority show little interest or concern (1967, page 29). Moreover, a further drift away from relating personnel departmental objectives to organizational ends occurs. It would appear that whereas their *goals* concentrate on programmes, personnel specialists' *time* is largely spent on day-to-day departmental administration and labour relations, neither of which they consider to be a major goal (page 31). Similarly, in a more recent investigation of a large organization's personnel specialists, a consultant commented, 'I found it difficult to guess what criteria people were using to decide how to structure their time. I often could not see how declared priorities and actual activities married up' (Honey, 1976, page 34). It would appear then that not only do personnel specialists abandon the attempt to demonstrate a direct relationship between specific organizational ends and their own departmental goals (i.e., the design and administration of personnel programmes), but that there also exists a disparity between their own goals and the activities they are chiefly engaged in.

Besides these confusions, other obstacles stand in the way of the personnel department's ability to demonstrate a relationship between its activities and organizational ends, as operationalized through its success criteria.

First, most would agree that personnel management, by definition, is chiefly concerned with the acquisition, maintenance and development of one of the resources (i.e., the human resource) through which organizational ends are achieved, rather than with the ends themselves. They are concerned with means rather than ends and inputs rather than outputs, and in situations where there is difficulty in determining the relationship between the two. This is for two reasons. As stated previously, personnel managers, by the very nature of their function, are dealing with a resource that cannot be manipulated as easily as inanimate objects. Compared with that relating to other factors of production (such as machinery or capital), the theory that explains the behaviour of the human factor is less developed, less systematic, and certainly less easy to apply in an organizational context, where there may be ethical objections to activities that smack of human engineering. Thus, the relationship between the effort and ability expended by the personnel manager and the achievement of *his* objectives (let alone organizational objectives) is often far less certain than it is for the production or engineering manager, for example, dealing with inanimate objects—except, of course, when these managers do in fact take on 'personnel' activities (e.g., when training, motivating, rewarding, and sanctioning their workforce). (Incidentally, it should perhaps be suggested at this point that recent comment (e.g., Toyne, 1976; Wilsher, 1976; Glover, 1976; Cairncross, 1976) about the low status of manufacturing/production in British industry could in part reflect the large personnel management component in production line management. In other words, the low status of manufacturing, *vis à vis* finance and marketing, for example, and particularly in labour intensive industries, could stem from production managers' failure to demonstrate success in meeting output and plant utilization targets, due to their 'personnel' problems of absenteeism, low effort levels, lack of labour flexibility, overtime bans, and strike action, etc.).

Moreover, because personnel is chiefly concerned with providing efficient inputs for use within other functional systems (e.g., those of sales, R and D, production, finance, and so on), not for use within its own system, the outputs these resources generate are achieved within, and are seen to be the achievement of these other systems. As discussed earlier, even if employees' ability to achieve required outputs is an indirect result of good personnel management in the areas of recruitment, training and development, and conditions of employment, the specific contribution of personnel is difficult to measure and isolate from effects of market and other organizational factors. The problem exists that, while a personnel department can measure its performance in terms of the number of activities undertaken—for example, the number of training and development courses run, the number of jobs evaluated, the production of a personnel manual itemizing conditions of employment, and personnel procedures—it can rarely, at present, demonstrate in quantifiable terms that X quantity and quality of these activities will have Y influence on employee behaviour, which in turn will contribute in Z degree to the achievement of a specific organizational end. One personnel manager, quoted in McFarland's AMA survey, summed up this problem as follows:

> Unfortunately we cannot say, 'I sold—dollars worth', or 'I designed the new product' or 'I built so many units'. Credit is hard to come by if you are effectively doing your job. Lack of turnover, improvement in supervision ability, and lessening of problems are perhaps negative. When you work in support of others, perhaps justifiably they are measured rather than you—unless your service is bad. Then of course, you get plenty of credit (1967, page 20).

Just as personnel managers tend to concern themselves more with 'means than ends, and activities rather than accomplishments (cf., Fischer, 1968, page 71), so too the difficulties in the situation give rise to a preference for measuring personnel outcomes in terms of the number and range of activities and programmes undertaken, and not, as Richardson comments, as 'business-impact variables' (1968). This approach, however, is ultimately self-defeating. Belief in activity for its own sake only encourages the unsophisticated personnel department to seek justification in the number of activities it encompasses, from the 'necessary chores' jettisoned by other functions, to the latest fashions in personnel programmes, regardless of their appropriateness to organizational needs. Activity for its own sake is likely to become a permanent substitute for undertaking analysis of what they, as personnel specialists, should be doing, and how they should evaluate the nature and outcomes of their activities as contributions to organizational ends. The failure to do this is likely to diminish the department's credibility and hence the resources it can generate in the long term. More seriously, lack of attention to ways of demonstrating the outcomes of activities. For it is admitted that developmental work is particularly even where, in contrast, a personnel department is undertaking sophisticated developmental work, such as a co-ordinated programme of OD activities. For, it is admitted that developmental work is particularly difficult to relate to conventional indicators of organizational success, not only because its potential results are difficult to measure in themselves and the time elapsed before they can come to fruition is lengthy, but because this time span often does not mesh with those over which the indicators of organizational success are to be measured.

However, failure to make any attempt to do this is to rely on the rest of management making an act of faith. While they may be prepared to do so in times of economic buoyancy, when levels of organizational slack are probably high, their faith is likely to be sustained only by the provision of hard economic results in times of economic recession. If these are not forthcoming, such developmental activities are likely to be starved of resources or even abandoned altogether, as they cannot be justified in terms of immediate return, nor often, incontrovertibly, demonstrate long-term benefits, even in terms of the programme in which they are set, let alone in terms of organizational ends. And this situation is self-perpetuating. If this happens, such half-hearted activities that do get off the ground are unlikely to convince the organization's policy-makers of the necessity of their survival and growth.

A case in point is provided by the history of management development activities at Company G, a medium sized engineering company, part of an international group of companies. Since 1966, three different management development schemes had been initiated in the company and each were considered by both personnel, line, and staff management groups to have been unsuccessful. This was attributed largely to an inability to resolve the potentially incompatible objectives sought at different levels and functions in the company; at group level and in the company's personnel department the emphasis being on management development as a means to facilitate closer integration among a diverse group of companies, at company plant level and among its line managers the emphasis shifting to appraisal as a means to improve short-term performance against financial criteria, in order to secure an increasing share of group resources. The failure of the last scheme seemed to be a result of the following, similar difficulties. First, the initiative for the system and its design had been largely a result of the involvement of the central personnel department, at group level, as at the time they were perceived by the company's central personnel department to have more expertise in this area and more resources in terms of time and personnel to devote to the exercise. Hence, at unit level (i.e., the constituent plants of Company G), it was seen by both line and personnel management as a 'bought-in' scheme concocted by personnel at group level, with the assistance of the central personnel department at company level, and one to which commitment was lacking from the start. Further, the scheme's rather tenuous connections with the operating level, together with the central personnel department's desire initially just to get some management development scheme in, before sorting out the major objectives of the scheme for each unit, resulted in different parties to it having different requirements and expectations, which did not become fully explicit until well into the process of implementation. The line, at unit level, felt it should be a mechanism for improving short-term performance, especially given the existing economic difficulties the company was facing. For example, they stated that its purpose should be to (a) enable people to perform their jobs more efficiently in the short run through the communication of standards both downwards and upwards, (b) enable succession analysis, (c) facilitate the 'better utilization of the time available to managers', and they wanted it to focus on success through the measurement of quantifiable results. Interestingly, they did not see it primarily as a device for identifying the training needs and highlighting the career expectations of individual managers. Central personnel, at group and company level, and to a lesser extent, the unit personnel managers, on the contrary, saw these 'developmental' objectives as paramount, along with that of enabling them to provide a better service function than existed (e.g., to assist them in systematizing the salary structure and making salary reviews more effective, to enable them to foresee gaps in recruitment, etc.). These conflicting objectives were further confused by the different priorities accorded to the line objectives in different plants which, together with the lack of internalization of the scheme at plant level, resulted in an impairment of data collection. Line managers tended to interpret what was required in the light of 'line' objectives generally and their own unit's priorities amongst these in particular, while the central personnel department attempted to use it in the light of theirs, leaving the unit personnel managers to reconcile the mismatches.

Not only was this a time-consuming exercise in itself, but given past failures, much of the basic groundwork such as job descriptions, the sorting out of accountabilities, devising new salary structures and organization charts, etc., had to be done again from scratch. As a result, a year after the exercise had started there had been no feedback at unit level on the information that had been collected at the first round of 'career assessment interviews' between individuals and their subordinates, nor on the new policies that these were leading up to. This lack of feedback, especially given the limited commitment to the scheme at unit level, and past failures, fostered a cynicism about the long-term benefits to be gained from it, and decreased motivation to co-operate whole heartedly in the next round of appraisal interviews, further devalueing the likely usefulness of such data, if obtained

It was in this context that after the scheme had been going for 18 months, its impetus was largely lost. As a result of the group's operating losses, the company began to cut back severely on employment, including its managerial staff. As a consequence, the resources of the group's and company's central personnel departments were cut, thus slowing down still further the rate at which basic groundwork to the scheme could be completed and feedback at unit level be undertaken. In view of redundancies and continuing high turnover of top management within the company, a general cynicism about personnel's conception of development grew amongst line managers at unit level, with a further decrease in their commitment to what was rapidly becoming another failed scheme.

This example highlights one of the main reasons why personnel specialists, in spite of the difficulties involved, need to evaluate their activities in terms similar to, or at least acceptable to, the rest of management. For, if line management has difficulty in accepting that long-term personnel programmes are a necessity rather than a luxury to be enjoyed when economic circumstances permit, then their commitment to their implementation, on a continuing basis, is likely to be problematic.

This relates directly to a second source of confusion when examining personnel's role in the achievement of organizational success which is, paradoxically, the 'omnipresent' nature of the personnel function. Not only does this give rise to difficulties in defining the boundaries between personnel and other management activities, but to the related problem of arriving at a realistic definition of what is, or should be, personnel's unique contribution. Thus, because every management function involves personnel activities, the personnel *department* cannot even lay an exclusive claim to those contributions to organizational success that the personnel *function* might claim, in particular to success in those 'personnel' activities that might be regarded as tangible and measurable. So 'strike free' production, low absenteeism, and labour turnover, all of which can be measured and might be accepted as indicators of the personnel function's indirect contribution to profitability, are not necessarily attributed to the personnel department and to personnel specialists.[21] For example, line managers

[21] This fact may in part explain the ambiguity reflected in a comment from the (American) IRI's report that

> The man directing his company's industrial relations/personnel program has mixed attitudes as to management's viewpoint on the function. On the one hand, he feels that the IR/P (industrial relations or personnel) department lacks status in comparison with other major elements of the company, and on the other, he believes, on the whole, that the value of the industrial relations/personnel function is recognized by management (see Herman, 1968, page 26).

frequently claim credit for, say, reduced absenteeism and labour turnover and often with justification, as such a state of affairs reflects the manner in which they have exercised the 'personnel' functions attached to their role. The necessary diffusion of aspects of the personnel function into line and other managerial functions, taken to its extreme, can lead to line management debating whether the personnel function needs an institutional presence at all.

Similarly, the involvement of other management functions in personnel work tends to undermine the status of the personnel specialist, as the work then does not appear to be a truly specialist activity involving unique knowledge and skills. It is too 'substitutable', to use Hickson *et al.*'s terms. Thus, Ritzer and Trice, on the basis of their research, commented:

> Corporate personnel was hindered by the fact that top management felt it knew more about personnel matters than the personnel department. This is unlike management's attitude towards other departments (e.g., engineering, accounting) in which management knows it does not have the expertise of these staff departments (1969, page 68).

The view that 'We all manage people, personnel is about managing people, hence anyone can (and does) undertake personnel work' was in the past, and still is, albeit to a lesser extent in the present, reinforced by the personnel department being used as 'a snug harbor for many an over-the-hill cast off who had been gently steered out of some other part of the organization' (Herman, 1968, page 24). This was certainly true in the case of Company F, the advertising company, for example, where responsibility for one of the major personnel functions (and of particular importance in that organizational context), management development, was ineffectively shared, on an *ad hoc* basis, between the line managers (account directors) and the heads of the various 'professional' departments (e.g., account planning, media, creative, representative) directly involved, resulting in a system based on patronage which lacked any attempt at a systematic coordination of career paths. In this organization the personnel director, the former company secretary, lacked both professional training in advertising (a source of legitimacy in the company) and in personnel management, was excluded from all the major policy and decision-making committees, and tended to be spoken of as existing chiefly to represent the 'social conscience' of the firm.

The omnipresent nature of personnel management can be understood in another sense. For, added to the problem discussed above, personnel specialists have to cope with a difficulty that arises in most line/staff relationships. That is, although the personnel department may be responsible for the design of various 'personnel' programmes or systems (e.g., job evaluation, management appraisal, wage and salary structure), their implementation must not only take place within other management systems, but largely involve the managers of these systems. Hence, the success or failure of a personnel programme, even within its own terms, is often removed from the direct control of the personnel specialists themselves. Lyons quotes a very obvious example of this problem:

> Recruitment is the work by which personnel departments in industry tend to be judged. This usually seems to them to be unfair because they cannot manufacture people, and they frequently feel that their failure to recruit is due more to management's refusal to accept their advice on personnel policy than their own incompetence at recruiting. . . . Few aspects of the personnel function show up fundamental weaknesses more clearly than does the problem of recruitment. If pay, conditions, structure etc., are wrong, recruitment will be difficult. If these things create labour turnover—as they will—recruitment will be doubly difficult because the number of vacancies is correspondingly increased. 'I'm merely pouring recruits into a sieve' is the *cri de coeur* of many a personnel officer upbraided because a host of unfilled vacancies is holding up production (1971, pages 37–38).

Similarly, it is a common phenomenon that managerial appraisal systems frequently founder through line management's reluctance to devote the time and effort necessary for successful implementation, quite apart from such deficiencies in design (e.g., a multiplicity of incompatible objectives) as may sap their motivation to do so.[22] Given these problems, not only is it difficult for personnel specialists to demonstrate a direct and exclusive contribution to the achievement of organizational ends, but often they are unable to claim that the activities they undertake are successful even in their own terms, irrespective of any indirect contribution to organizational success. This difficulty in demonstrating success, in either functional or organizational terms, may result in the regressive situations described above, in which their lack of expertise, credibility, resources and, hence, power within the organisation becomes self-perpetuating.

Conclusion

Confronted by a difficulty in demonstrating success in both functional and organizational terms, the authority of a personnel department and the specialists within it is constantly undermined. Hence the frequent complaint that personnel systems, such as those of management appraisal and development, are not taken as seriously as they 'should' be by line management, who go through the motions of support without much appreciation or commitment to what the specialists involved are trying to

---

[22] Cf., the finding of an IPM (1973) survey on management appraisal in British firms (N = 360) that 'only about half the companies appear to recognize the importance of training line managers in appraisal interviewing—an area which is notoriously susceptible to human error and mishandling' (Gill *et al.*, page 10). Incidentally, this survey shows how far from the prescriptions of the standard textbooks management appraisal practices still are, in general, in British companies.

achieve.[23] Hence, too, the reported refusal of line management in the engineering industry to delegate responsibilities for procedural matters at the various formal conferences to personnel specialists (Marsh, 1971); the impression of some trade unionists 'that all too often, personnel managers have no real authority to reach settlement . . . (which) imparts an air of unreality to negotiations' (Jenkins, 1973, page 34); and the recent research finding that, at plant level, both managers, shop stewards, and other workers' representatives in the locations studied rarely sought the advice of personnel officers on points of labour relations practice (Poole, 1973, 1976). Also, the conclusion drawn by Ritzer and Trice, not only from their case study, but from a nation-wide survey of American personnel managers, that while personnel managers felt they could make decisions, they did not feel that they had the authority to carry them out (1969, page 74). Added to this, there is Miner's recent research results, that personnel and industrial relations managers appear to have less motivation to manage than other managerial groups and that 'their lack of assertiveness is so pervasive as to suggest a defining characteristic of the field' (1976, page 419). In these circumstances, it is not surprising that personnel specialists often fail to be included in major company policy-making forums even if the decisions taken there may have far-reaching implications for personnel policy. Or, if they are included, it is usually in the role of facilitator to many policy decisions already taken, providing, for example, information on the availability of the right quantity and quality of labour to implement (and its likely reactions to) policies that have largely been decided. In this situation, the personnel department all too easily becomes the organization's scapegoat function.

How can personnel specialists break out of this vicious circle of lack of authority, denial of information and support, low levels of expertise and credibility, inability to demonstrate success, diminished authority, and so on?

The next two chapters consider strategies by which they may seek to rectify this situation.

[23]Cf., the following comment from Herman:

> A 1961 study by the industry serving Opinion Research Corporation revealed that despite the ringing endorsements of their highest company executives on the subject of manager development, when plant managers were asked in the privacy of their own office, and with a guarantee of anonymity, what they thought were their major responsibilities, the development and training of managers was near the bottom of their lists.
> Near the top were production scheduling and cost and budget control. Recollecting our earlier discussion on the big measurement push, this is not surprising. Production scheduling and cost and budget control are quantifiable as can be, but how would you measure and put incentive bonus points on the development of one or two, or half a dozen future managers? . . . In most cases, the combination of a natural lack of enthusiasm for systematic manager education and the press of more immediate profit oriented concerns by the middle levels of the corporate structure would, if left unchecked, ultimately kill off the majority of management development throughout the country (1968; pages 166–167).

APPENDIX I

The following provides a brief outline[1] of the companies from whose case studies illustrative material has been drawn

	SIZE (No's Employed in Company Overall)[2]	TECHNOLOGY (Woodward's Classification[3])	INDUSTRY	Level of Organization at which Data Collected (National HQ, Divisional HQ, Plant Level)
Company A	Large	Process	Oil	National HQ, Operating Plants
Company B	Large	Process	Petro-Chemicals	Divisional HQ, Operating Plants
Company C	Medium	Large Batch/Mass Prod	Engineering	National HQ, An Operating Plant
Company D	Medium	Process	Animal Feeds	National HQ, An Operating Plant
Company E	Medium	Process	Pharmaceuticals	Divisional HQ, Operating Plants
Company F	Small	Unit	Advertising	National HQ, An Operating Plant
Company G	Medium	Large Batch	Engineering	National and Divisional HQs, Operating Plants
Company H	Large	Process	Chemicals	Divisional HQ, Operating Plant
Company I	Medium	Routine/Service	Leisure/Entertainments	National and Divisional HQs, Operating Plants
Company J	Large	Unit/Small Batch	Engineering	National HQ, Operating Plants

[1] These details are intended to provide only an indicator of the types of companies involved in the case study research, on which the conclusions drawn are based. In no sense, as will be clear from Chapter VI, are they adequate or intended to represent organizational context in its technical sense.

[2] Below 2 000 employees = Small; Above 2 000, Below 12 000 = Medium; Above 12 000 = Large. It should be noted that if a ratio between average numbers employed and net company assets was compiled, a slightly different picture would emerge, as Company E had a substantially above average level of assets for numbers employed, while Company J had a substantially below average level of assets for numbers employed. This again calls into question uni-dimensional measurements of company characteristics.

[3] Excluding Company I.

4. The search for authority: the conformist and deviant innovator

How can the personnel function, in its broadest sense, gain a higher priority in organizational decision-making? How can a personnel manager increase the power his department exercises within an organization? Although logically distinct, these two questions are related, and their consideration provides a starting point for this chapter.

The personnel function: pressures for its higher priority in decision-making and implementation

What is likely to give the 'personnel' dimension, involved in all managerial decisions and activities, greater weight than in the recent past? Over the last few years, and with increasing momentum, environmental and organizational changes have taken place which, in Hickson *et al.*'s (1971) terms, have generated uncertainties, whose resolution (while essential to organizational success) depends on the development and use of personnel management expertise. The major problematic areas which have been identified by a range of commentators (e.g., Myers, 1971; Thomason, 1975; Margerison, 1976a) may be summarized as follows:

Legislative developments. In the last decade, legislation affecting the relationship between employer and employee has proliferated, and set very real constraints on management's freedom to operate unfettered in both the organization's internal and external labour markets. The wide range and scope of the legislation is indicated by the following list compiled by Margerison (1976a, page 42), viz.,

The Contract of Employment Act
Health and Safety at Work Act
Redundancy Acts
Equal Pay Act
Industrial Training Acts
Trade Union and Labour Relations Act
The Industry Act
The Employment Protection Act
Prices and Incomes Legislation
Sex Discrimination Act

This phenomenon of increased government intervention, which largely reflects changes in social values, is common to most western industrialized countries (in relation to Europe, see, for example, Stewart, 1976). Even in the USA, where free enterprise philosophies are perhaps even more firmly entrenched than in Europe, comparable legislative intervention regulating employment conditions has recently taken place, notably in the form of the Office of Federal Contract Compliance (OFCC) and the Equal Opportunities Commission (EEOC) Affirmative Action Programs, together with such legislation as the Occupational Safety and Health Act, the Age Discrimination in Employment Act, and the Employee Retirement Income Security Act (see, e.g., Glueck, 1974, pages 537–55; Chayes, 1974; Purcell, 1974; Buckley, 1975; Cook, 1975; Churchill and Shank, 1976). In Great Britain's case, moreover, the increase in legislation has been further accelerated by the need to bring conditions of employment into line with EEC requirements (Owen, 1976), while at the same time battling with inflation levels higher than its competitors'. Even bearing in mind the inevitable loopholes in the law and slippages between legislation and implementation (cf., Pressman and Wildavsky, 1973; *Personnel Management*, April 1976, page 13; *Personnel Management*, September 1976, page 7; *Personnel Management*, December, 1976, page 5), such government intervention has not only placed direct constraints on management's freedom to manage the employment relationship (generally in negotiation with its employees) as it thinks fit, but indirectly it has increased the cost of labour, and consequently the necessity for its efficient utilization. Theoretically, this process is likely to increase the focus on human resources in that there will be the need for more 'management' of them. For example, when it becomes too costly to make labour redundant owing to the financial penalties contained in legislation, it is likely that programmes of retraining, combined with more attention to manpower planning and recruitment policy, may be undertaken. (For detailed analysis of the implications of the British legislation for personnel management in general, and personnel specialists in particular see, for example, Thomason, 1976, chapter 11 (a general survey); Mepham, 1974; Buckingham, 1974; Pettman, 1975; Aitken, 1976; Rubenstein and Frost, 1977 (Equal Pay); Wainwright, 1975, (Sex Discrimination Act); Rubenstein, 1975; Roots, 1975; Kessler and Palmer, 1975; Scouller, 1975; Cowan, 1975 (Employment Protection Act); Mumford, 1975; Daniel, 1976 (Redundancy Acts); Thomason, 1976, chapter 6; Weekes *et al.*, 1975 (Industrial Relations legislation).

Increased militancy on the part of blue-collar unions. Not only have the number of disputes risen in the past decade, but the number of days lost *per* dispute have risen too[1] (*Monthly Digest of Statistics*, 1975). To some extent this has been linked to the growth in plant bargaining, which on the one hand has encouraged settlements compatible with local labour market conditions, and on the other provoked resulting claims that inter-plant differentials have been upset and that parity should either be established or re-established. In periods of economic buoyancy, this has tended to encourage inter-plant leapfrogging (which has fed into intra-plant differentials disputes), while in periods of recession and incomes restraint, it has provoked disputes over unresolved parity and differentials claims that may act as a trigger to explosive demands and prolonged disputes when government controls are temporarily lifted.

Further, militancy has been expressed in new types of challenge to managerial prerogatives, viz., the 'sit-in' or 'work-in' activities of union groups who refuse to accept managerially prescribed redundancy, and in a few cases even attempt to substitute workers' control in place of close-down (Mills, 1976; Eccles, 1977).

The organization of white-collar, technical, and managerial staff. Not only is this group the fastest growing in the labour force, but it is rapidly overcoming its traditional reluctance to organize into unions·(as opposed to staff associations and professional bodies). Several reasons have been identified for this development, some structural (for example, the increasing degree of concentration of employment), some procedural (for example, government policies promoting union recognition as in the Trade Union and Labour Relations Act, the degree to which employers are then prepared to recognize such unions for purposes of negotiation) (Bain,

---

[1] Some commentators have seen an indirect relationship here with legislative enactments, e.g., that strikers, even without strike pay, can support themselves for relatively long periods through the provision of supplementary benefits, tax rebates and so on (Gennard and Lasko, 1975).

It should be noted, though, that in the past year (1975–1976), with the rise of unemployment and the TUC's and major unions' support of the Government's incomes policy, the number of disputes and days lost through disputes has fallen. However, it is doubtful whether this fall will be maintained once full employment is re-established, especially in the light of the differentials claims that are being fostered by the 'rough justice' of the existing incomes policy.

1970), and some in the economic circumstances of the past decade (Bamber, 1976). In this period, the pay differentials between technical and supervisory staff on the one hand and that of manual workers on the other have been largely eroded, first by productivity bargaining, and subsequently by 'flat-rate' incomes policies. Similarly, managerial staff have recently experienced a substantial drop in their real incomes both through their observance of incomes policies and increased rates of taxation (Newbould *et al.*, 1976). For both groups, at the same time, there has been a perceived erosion of occupational status resulting in what Wright Mills (1951) has termed 'status panic'. Supervisors have found portions of their jobs lost to their subordinates on the one hand, through programmes of job enrichment, and to their superordinates on the other, as discretion at plant level is curtailed through standardized procedures and centralization in decision-making. Growth in plant bargaining has further undermined their position as the increasingly powerful shop-stewards have by-passed them as a communication channel and worked directly with management. At the same time, middle managements have felt themselves under pressure: computerization has removed some of the discretion previously exercised, as have policies of centralization and participation, while the manager no longer feels immune from an experience previously confined to the shop floor, i.e., redundancy (Wood, 1975). Further, while managerial prerogatives and privileges seem under attack, recent legislation has increased his level of personal responsibility. For example, 'in the eyes of a factory inspector, a manager may stand in the employer's shoes as his representative, and he is liable to be prosecuted individually under the current health and safety legislation' (Bamber, 1976; Health and Safety at Work Act, 1974, Sections 36 and 37).

In these circumstances, militancy is likely to increase in traditionally 'loyal' sections of the labour force, as has been evidenced by recent action in the public sector.

The implementation of and adaptation to organizational change. The three factors listed above all add up to the fact that labour costs are an increasingly significant area of total costs and, as such, the resource they purchase must be utilized as efficiently as possible. This may involve such strategies as the substitution of capital for labour as in technological investment, the introduction of new control systems, the redesign of jobs, the more flexible use of labour, and so on. In all cases, but especially in that of technological change, with its far-reaching implications for job content, job security, retraining, the re-organization of working arrangements and authority structures and so on, there is a need to negotiate the acceptance of change with the employees involved and provide whatever training and development is required (not to mention the implications for manpower planning, wage and salary structures, etc.). A change programme is unlikely to prove successful if the requirements and expectations

72

of the employees involved are treated as the least significant and least problematic variable in the situation (Likert, 1967; Bennis *et al.*, 1969).

The changing nature of employees' expectations about the employment relationship. As is implicit in the factors mentioned above, employees increasingly have more demanding expectations of the work situation. Partly as a result of societal development (in education and, generally, in the development of the welfare state), partly as a result of the 'tight' labour markets of the 1960s, and partly as a result of pressure generated by the organizations themselves (as in their marketing policies, that through advertising express the supreme value of consumption), employees have grown to expect regular increases in the real purchasing power of their wages and salaries, a progressively shorter working week (or an increasing proportion of hours worked at premium rates), and a 'better' physical working environment. They are less willing to tolerate poor working conditions whether expressed in low pay, long hours, dirty, heavy, or repetitive work (unless adequately compensated), or the arbitrary exercise of managerial prerogatives, inappropriate to present social values, without taking collective or individual industrial action. Such attitudes on the part of potential employees are not only an important factor in the increased labour costs discussed earlier (and hence, in a general sense, contribute to the need to utilize an increasingly costly resource as efficiently as possible), but directly involve consideration of the adequacy of traditional methods of consultation and decision-making, of styles of management, the organization of work and design of jobs, and so on (Davis and Cherns, 1975; Butteriss, 1971; Wall and Lischeron, 1977). In particular, this has recently been expressed in the widespread recognition, by government, union (TUC) and employer (CBI) representatives, of the need for greater industrial democracy, and the continuing debate as to what form this should take (Bullock Report, 1977).

Summary. These five factors, logically, should necessitate that the personnel function, both in theory and in practice, achieves a higher priority in organizational decision-making, irrespective of the development of its institutionalized presence, the personnel department. (Indeed, there are some indicators, such as personnel managers at last catching up other managerial groups, in salary terms (see Inbucon/AIC Management Consultants Ltd., *Survey of Executive Salaries and Fringe Benefits*, 1975, 1976), that this is happening). This is because all the developments listed above imply that labour costs are not only becoming higher absolutely, but are becoming and will become a higher proportion of total costs, if attention is not paid to the efficient utilization and development of the resource they represent. In these circumstances, even if it is still difficult to demonstrate the direct contribution of *good* personnel management to the achievement of organizational goals as measured by financial success criteria, it is relatively easy to show that *inadequate* personnel management carries heavy financial costs.

In other words, not only is the management of human resources involving more uncertainties, or problematic issues, *per se*, but the financial implications involved make coping with them of vital importance to the organization, given the prevalent financial nature of the success criteria employed. Hence, not only is the personnel function, in its broadest sense, by an increase in its perceived 'centrality', likely to assume more prominence in organizational decision-making, but the personnel department too is theoretically likely to increase its power. The developments outlined above may be seen to offer the personnel department the opportunity to control contingencies 'strategic' to the organization, *if* it can first develop an exclusive (i.e., 'non-substitutable') expertise.

The personnel department's relationship to this development. In the previous section, it was argued that the developments outlined *logically* should give rise to the personnel function as a whole being treated as a higher priority than at present. However, this logic holds only if the managements involved actually *do* perceive that these developments are taking place and that they have important financial implications. In theory, this is where the personnel department should seize the opportunity to draw the rest of management's attention to the implications of these developments and, having done so, negotiate an enhanced position in the organization on the basis of their ability to control contingencies that are now agreed as strategic to the organization's survival and growth. In practice, of course, personnel departments often fail to carry out either activity successfully, because of their members' initial lack of credibility with other management groups. Thus, even when circumstances are conducive to personnel departments achieving more power, they cannot be fully exploited unless the department has already gained a measure of credibility. But, the question remains, how can this be done from an initially low power base within the organization?

Personnel specialists, recognizing this problem, have tended to tackle it by looking for a power base outside the confines of the organization (but with strong links into it), drawing support from recognition on a wider basis. This strategy has been expressed in the frequent cry that what personnel really needs is to become more 'professional', that those who wish to work as personnel specialists 'should' have their own 'professional' qualifications and that these should be underwritten by the development of an examining and self-regulating 'professional' body (such as IPM in the UK). For as one commentator has stated:

A guarantee goes with being 'professional'. It is not an extravagant one . . . but professionalism does ensure legitimacy at a minimum level, anyway (Herman, 1968, page 32).

Yet, because the rallying cry of 'professionalism' is surrounded by a confusion of definitional problems, beneath its banner have arisen two different approaches to the quest for authority, between which, although they sit uneasily together, personnel managers oscillate, as neither is fully viable. The next sections of this chapter therefore discuss the concept of professionalism in relation to these two alternative approaches.

The nature of professionalism

What, then, is professionalism? A long and unresolved debate continues around the definitions and appropriate use of such concepts as 'profession', 'professionalism' and 'professionalization' (Jackson, 1970; Johnson, 1972; Daniels, 1975). This both reflects and arises out of the confusion that surrounds our everyday use of the term 'professional'. For example, is the term meant to indicate that an *occupation* possesses certain characteristics or that the *individuals* employed perform their jobs in a certain manner? This is the implicit distinction made when, on the one hand, we talk of the 'medical profession', yet equally talk of a 'professional' entertainer or footballer. In the latter sense, the adjective is often equated with the noun, and a 'professional' means no more than an individual with almost any kind of expertise. Suffice it to say here, though, that the concepts of 'profession' and 'professionalism' have generally been examined from two major perspectives, which have contrasting implications for personnel specialists in their search for greater authority.

The first approach has been to ask what list of attributes represents the common core of professional occupations (e.g., Carr Saunders and Wilson, 1933; Greenwood, 1957; Barber, 1963; Millerson, 1964). Many different lists have been compiled to produce a 'trait' model of what constitutes a profession, and although there is no consensus as to what the crucial elements are, the most frequently mentioned traits are (1) skill based on theoretical knowledge; (2) the provision of training and education; (3) testing the competence of members/peer group evaluation of competence; (4) organization i.e., a professional culture is sustained by formal professional associations, which have the power to regulate entry to (and, sometimes, promotion within) the profession; (5) adherence to a professional code of conduct, and (6) altruistic service.[2] 'Professionalism' is

---

[2] Cf., for example, the list of traits compiled by Barber, who distinguishes four essential attributes of professional behaviour (a) generalized knowledge; (b) primary orientation to the community interest; (c) internalized code of ethics; (d) rewards which primarily symbolize work achievement. Or the criteria Greenwood isolates as delineating a profession, viz., (1) a systematic body of theory requiring lengthy training; (2) a professional authority leaving the client no choice but to accept professional judgement; (3) professional control over admission to the field; (4) a regulative code of ethics which actually compels correct behaviour from members; (5) a professional culture distinct from that, or not possessed by, other occupational groups. It may be argued that the bulk of these characteristics involves less what tasks professionals do than the manner in which they perform them, hence the confusion between noun and adjective noted earlier.

then seen as the ideology that characterizes occupations possessing those traits—in other words 'professions' (Johnson, 1972, pages 23–24).[3]

Generally speaking, in this model, the essential trait an occupation must possess to claim professional status is that of a high level of technical expertise, of a type valued by, and to be utilized largely at the behest of the client. The professional is then often the expert who works within the client's brief, critical if it appears inappropriate, but not primarily motivated to rewrite it.

A second approach has been to define 'professionalism' less in terms of the distinguishing characteristics of a particular occupation than as a way of controlling an occupation.[4] As Johnson puts it:

> Professionalism, then, becomes redefined as a peculiar type of occupational control rather than an expression of the inherent nature of particular occupations. A profession is not then, an occupation, but a means of controlling an occupation (1972, page 45).

In other words, if occupational control is seen in terms of the characteristic way in which the tensions in the producer (i.e., professional)—consumer (i.e., client) relationship are resolved, *then professionalism may be considered as existing in situations where the producer is able to define the needs of the consumer and the manner in which these needs are to be met.* In other words, the essence of professionalism may be seen in terms of a particular type of authority relationship existing between the 'professional' and his client.

What, then, is the nature of a professional's authority? Freidson (1968), building on earlier work by Hughes (1958), has explored this question, through a comparison with that of the scientist. A scientist deals with colleagues who share his premises and basic knowledge and who are inclined to accept his findings (i.e., be influenced by him) when they conform to common rules of evidence and procedure. In other words, 'authority here is based on persuasion grounded in a common universe of discourse, a shared set of paradigms' (Freidson, 1968, page 27). In contrast, because a professional seeks to exert authority over lay clients, this authority cannot rest on the persuasion of competent advice. The very notion of a client implicitly inhibits persuasion. A client differs from a

---

[3] Several commentators have questioned the validity of this 'attribute' approach. For example, it has been suggested that this approach to deriving a definition of 'professionalism' relies too heavily on the views of 'professionals' themselves, without serious attempt to discover if the statements they make can be empirically verified. Is long training really necessary for some professions or has it become an artefact for advancing status and controlling entry? It is thus argued that the attribute approach can lead researchers to neglect the relationship between behaviour and ideology, to fail to recognize the process of 'career straightening' (Hughes, 1971), and so on (see Daniels, 1975).

[4] It may be noted that Greenwood's criteria for delineating a profession, listed before, are very much concerned with those attributes that have implications for control, whether control of professionals by their peers, or of the relationship between the professional and his client. Hence, although the two approaches may be treated as distinct, there is a measure of overlap, at least by implication.

customer (or for that matter from a colleague) in that while the latter determines what services or commodities he wants, on the premise that he has the capacity to appraise his own needs and judge which potential service or commodity would satisfy them, the client has no choice but to accede to 'professional' judgement, on the premise that because he lacks the requisite theoretical background, he cannot diagnose his own needs or discriminate among the possibilities for meeting them.[5] (Hence, the customary view of the established professions that it is unethical for individuals within the profession to advertise their services, as it may impute to the potential client the discriminating capacity to select from competing forms of the same service). Thus, as far as the judgement of an individual professional's competence goes, this remains firmly in the hands of his peers, when judgement then conforms to the pattern of one scientist judging another. The client, on the contrary, is expected to attribute competence to the profession as a whole, rather than to its individual members as such. But if the professional does not gain his authority over his client on the basis of persuasion, whence does it arise? Freidson argues that:

> the solution of the professional is to have himself designated as the expert in such a way as to exclude all other claimants, his designation being official and bureaucratic as formally established by law (1968, page 28).[6]

In other words, 'professional authority' stems from the fact that society gives to certain 'professional' groups the exclusive legal right to operate and control the access to goods and services which a layman (the potential client) is likely to feel he needs in order even to manage his own problem himself, independently of expert advice. For example, in Great Britain, an individual is not normally compelled to seek a registered doctor's advice in the treatment of any illness he may suffer, yet without a doctor's signed prescription form, he is unable to obtain many of the medicines he needs to treat himself. Ultimately, too, only a registered doctor can sign a death certificate. *The more strategic the accessories controlled by a profession, then,*

---

[5] Of course, this is to employ an ideal type model of professional authority. In practice, the authority of the professional is nowhere near as absolute, for even the patient will question the unpalatable opinions of the most eminent medical specialist. Generally speaking, though, the more essential the service the professional offers, and the more monopolistic the level of control, the greater the chance that this professional authority will exist; the more discretionary the service, and the less monopolistic the control on entrants to the profession, the less likely is it to exist (see also the subsequent discussion).

[6] This designation, however, may be based on persuasion. As Freidson comments:

> It seems quite correct to characterize as a kind of persuasion the way the leaders of an occupation influence the establishment to create and maintain it as a profession ... The leaders of an occupation persuade leaders of society that its members possess some technical competence so special and of such importance that the public should be prevented from using any other occupation with the same domain but assertedly lesser competence or integrity. The formal, institutionalized status of a profession is granted by society on the basis of having been persuaded that an occupation is competent and responsible (1968, page 32).

the stronger the sanctions supporting its authority. As Freidson summarizes the situation, at the level of interaction between the client and the professional, the latter's authority is based not on the 'persuasion of the competence of advice on the basis of available evidence, but rather (on) a closing-off of alternatives to the client so that he has little choice but to go to the practitioner, and (on) a reliance upon the authority of incumbency in a status to which competence has been imputed' (1968, page 32). Thus, Freidson's argument that the control of 'strategic accessories' lies at the root of professional authority, in fact echoes earlier comments on the relationship between a function's substitutability and centrality and the power it can acquire.

Now, clearly, this model of professional authority is more of an ideal type model, based on professional occupations in their most highly developed form, than one which can be applied directly to personnel specialists groping after some form of professional identity. However, it does suggest that there are two basic steps that have to be taken by members of occupations aspiring to professional status, as a means of controlling the producer–consumer relationship. The first is that an occupation has to demonstrate its competence in a particular area before society will grant it the professional's 'licence to practise', or quasi-monopolistic control over the provision of certain goods or services. Consequently, aspirants to professional status are still in the business of persuasion until this status has been achieved for their occupation. The second step is that the individual wishing to practice in this field has then to be certified as fit to do so by fellow professionals employing standards based on a body of systematic theory and up-to-date practise. The candidate has to persuade his colleagues that he is competent, even if, having done so, he no longer has to convince his clients.

This pinpoints the basic problem the personnel specialist has to confront if he aspires to this model of professionalism. That is, to what extent can the other managerial groups that the personnel specialist has to work with ever really see themselves as his clients, in the sense understood by the 'true' professional? Not only might they question their 'lay' status (even if they admit to lacking specifically 'personnel' expertise they are still 'managers') but their own involvement in personnel management, in its broad sense, might convince them that the model of a colleague relationship (the 'scientific' rather than 'professional' model) might be more appropriate. Similarly, it is less society as such that can grant 'professional' bodies such as the IPM the right to certify managers as 'professional' personnel specialists, than the major employing organizations. Can the managers who run these organizations really be both validators of personnel specialists' professional status and clients of these same people?

In these circumstances, although these two contrasting approaches to professionalism lie at the root of two strategies personnel specialists have adopted to reinforce and augment such authority as they already possess, it is not surprising that the more widely favoured strategy, which may be termed *'conformist' innovation*, derives from the less problematic model of professionalism, that is, the 'trait' model.

'Conformist' innovation

This occurs when the personnel specialist defines his professionalism in terms of *acquiring expertise that will enable him to demonstrate a closer relationship between his activities (means) and organizational success criteria (ends)* (cf., Merton, 1957). Therefore, he accepts the dominant utilitarian values and bureaucratic relationships within the organization and tries to demonstrate the worth of his activities within this framework. This generally involves a two-faceted approach.

Although the difficulties in the way of establishing a direct relationship between his department's work and the achievement of organizational objectives may prove insurmountable, the personnel specialist may attempt to highlight his department's role in indirectly facilitating organizational success by tackling potentially costly impediments to it (e.g., by taking action to reduce levels of labour turnover, by designing a career structure to minimize potential management succession problems, and so on). Thus, the emphasis is shifted. Personnel's contribution to the achievement of organizational success becomes less important than its role in anticipating, preventing, or rectifying a range of malfunctions.

As such, personnel specialists tend to emphasize not their advisory relationships with other managerial groups—for useful advice has a habit of becoming the property of the recipient and, unlike 'bad' advice, its origins lost in the allocation of praise—but, in Sayles' (1964) terminology, their 'auditing' and 'stabilization' relationships. 'Auditing' relationships may be described as those that involve ascertaining whether the various managerial functions' activities are consistent with specified organizational rules or standards, while 'stabilization' relationships are those that involve granting prior approval to the critical decisions of these groups, on the basis of a specialist expertise that also takes into consideration the total organization's needs in this area. Hence, they are relationships designed to cope bureaucratically with problems of control and co-ordination *via* scrutiny before, during, and after the event. Therefore, as far as personnel management is concerned, both these relationships involve their specialists in minimizing the danger and the cost of potentially inconsistent and inappropriate decision-making on the part of other managerial groups, as it may effect human resource issues (cf., Foulkes and Morgan, 1977). For example, attempts to monitor whether a performance appraisal pro-gramme is working as designed (auditing) and to ensure that decisions about managerial promotion and remuneration are sanctioned prior to implementation (stabilization) so that differentials problems will not be created through ignorance or by default, can both be justified as preventing potentially costly mistakes that might otherwise undermine organizational effectiveness.

The general attention to cost is underlined by the other facet of this approach. That is, there develops an appreciation on the part of personnel specialists that their contribution will appear more tangible if presented in financial terms.[7] So they now attempt to measure the success of their activities in the same cost-effectiveness terms as other managerial groups. This has stimulated an interest in two related developments: human resource accounting (Cheek, 1972) and quantitative and OR based techniques involving computer-based data processing and information systems (Greenlaw and Smith, 1970).

Human resource accounting. In a literal sense, 'human resource accounting' means the measurement of the cost and value of people to organizations. More generally, it can refer to the process of identifying, measuring, and communicating information about human resources to decision-makers (Flamholtz, 1974). As far as personnel specialists are concerned (as opposed to those interested in the theory of accounting), HRA has two major objectives. First, the development and use of measures of human resource cost[8] and value[9] allows decisions about the acquisition, develop-

---

[7] Superficially, the personnel specialist may appear to seek both charismatic authority and that derived from conformist innovation by combining both approaches. Thus, he may attempt to sell to the Board 'panaceas' that reputedly will increase job satisfaction and decrease industrial unrest overnight and so contribute visibly to organizational profitability. It is in this context that we should understand personnel specialists' often-reported interest in magical formulae and 'gimmicks', (Drucker, 1961, page 269; Herman, 1968, page 303; Klein, 1976, pages 185–186). However, the resemblance of 'persuasion through panaceas' to the conformist innovation strategy is more apparent than real as, in these circumstances, the personnel manager may place more reliance on his *persuasive* abilities than on his professional *technical competence* to 'validate' the claims he makes for his activities' value to the organization.

[8] Three different concepts have been proposed for the measurement of human resource costs: original cost (i.e., the actual historical outlay incurred as an investment in human resources), replacement cost (the cost that would be incurred today to replace an organization's human resources), and opportunity cost (the maximum amount that human resources could earn in an alternative use, the figure to be arrived at by a system of competitive bidding for the resource in question). For further discussion of these measures, see Brummet, Flamholtz and Pyle, 1968, 1969; Flamholtz, 1973; Hekimian and Jones, 1967).

[9] Theoretically, the value of people to an organization is the present worth of future service they are expected to render. Yet, in order to account for the effects of synergism, it is necessary to develop different methods for valuing different aggregations of human resources: indivduals, groups, and the total human organization.

To measure a resource's value, it is necessary to forecast its expected service life (the valuation period) and estimate its expected future services. For a monetary valuation, expected future services must be translated into monetary terms and discounted to their present value. Suggested methods include 'the adjusted discounted future wages method' (Hermanson, 1964), 'discounted future compensation method' (Lev and Schwartz, 1971, 1972), 'the stochastic process with service rewards' (Flamholtz, 1971), mainly used to assess individual valuations, and that of Brummet, Flamholtz and Pyle (1968), based on the changes in a firm's present value attributable to human resources, used to measure a group's value.

In a non-monetary valuation, the forecast of expected future services is equivalent to measuring the resource's subjective expected utility (Edwards, 1962).

ment, allocation, compensation, and replacement of human resources to be facilitated by assessing the costs to be incurred and the value derived from various actions and activities. For example, a decision involving the possible investment in skills training could be assessed in terms of its expected monetary return on investment. Second, this provides a method by which the effectiveness of management's utilization of this resource can be monitored and evaluated by assessing the extent to which it has appreciated, conserved, or depleted human resources. Thus, for example, it would be possible to measure the loss of human capital attributable to turnover, for when turnover occurs, it could be calculated by this method the extent to which the unamortized investment in people is lost and the opportunity cost incurred of unrealized human value. This, it is argued, gives a better indication of the economic significance of turnover compared with the straight turnover rates generally used at present.

Human Resource Accounting tends to be applied in organizations in two ways (Flamholtz, 1974). The first, more ambitious way is through the development of systems of accounting for human resource costs or value. For example, the R. G. Barry Corporation accounts for its investments in human resources and attempts to assess the rate at which these investments are more or less productive than others. As such, the system is primarily intended to provide information to facilitate decision-making involving human resources and to provide feedback to managers on their performance in utilizing this resource. The company's management reports that the system is used in manpower planning, strategic planning, and management control (Woodruff, 1970).

The second approach is to apply HRA on a problem-oriented basis. For example, it can be used to assess the real costs of redundancy and turnover, to estimate appropriate levels of training in the light of organizational objectives, to assess the value of assessment programmes, and so on. Examples of its use in this way can be found in Flanders (1971), Giles and Robinson (1972), and Stewart and Stewart (1976, chapter 9).

Clearly, however, HRA is still in an embryonic stage of development (both theoretically and in application) and has a long way to go before it can be used as an everyday technique by personnel and accounting specialists, let alone become part of the way of thinking of management in general (Strauss, 1976; Craft and Birnberg, 1976; Rhode, Lawler and Sundem, 1976). Theoretically, there do seem to be some inconsistencies in a concept that can embrace both an evaluation of total assets based on historical costs and an evaluation of the future returns on present or projected investment. Conceptually, the underlying assumption behind all the methods, that it is an advantage to have well-trained and high-cost people, may be at variance with the usual business objective to be maximally profitable with a minimum of assets and costs, and with the usual (British) business practice, compounded by banking conventions, of putting a higher priority on short-term profitability, in response to shareholders demands, rather than on long-term investment and growth. Practically, there are numerous problems to be ironed out in application. For example, there is the use of HRA in a redundancy situation where the objective is to minimize the loss of undepreciated investment. It has been argued that while, in theory, a reduction of skilled people would lead to a reduction in the total stock of human capital, if, as a result, profitability improved, the stock market and shareholders might 'unanimously react by moving the market capitalization sharply upward as the profit effect was identified' (Courtis, 1973), in which case, using a multiplier method, the value of the people left, on paper at least, might be greater. This is an example of apparently opposite answers arising from two different methods. These and other reservations about the real usefulness of HRA have been voiced by Cannon (1974a, 1974b), for example.

Clearly, for HRA to become a source of expert power open to the personnel specialist (or to the accountant interested in developing the organization's personnel function), these problems must be tackled. Otherwise, their credibility will again be questioned and the view may prevail that, lacking the expertise to evaluate the practical utility of new techniques and approaches to management, personnel tends to fall for the latest gimmicks, involving the organization in either unnecessary costs or positively harmful exercises. But, in spite of these caveats, HRA does focus attention on the financial implications of human resource management, on the idea 'that people are a resource that should be considered as valuable and therefore utilized as such rather than an unmeasurable factor of production' (Cannon, 1974a, page 20). As such, not only does it offer techniques by which personnel specialists can demonstrate an expertise within the same frame of reference as that employed by financial specialists (perhaps the most powerful group in organizations today, involved as they are in the privileged task of arbitrating means–ends relationships), but it also stimulates management's recognition of the economic importance of the personnel function throughout the organization. This could have a spill-over effect on the status of what are often seen as routine personnel activities, for, as Flamholtz comments:

> If the aim of human resource management is seen as the optimization of human resource value, (and if this can be measured in financial terms) then task design, selection, role assignment, development, performance appraisal, and compensation are not merely a set of service functions to be performed; rather they are a set of available strategies that can be adopted to change the value of human assets and, in turn, the value of the organization as a whole (Flamholtz, 1971).

In these circumstances, organizations might well be prepared to invest more resources in, demand higher standards of performance and allocate more rewards in terms of pay, status and power to their personnel departments.

Quantitative techniques and computerized information systems. In many of the case study firms referred to earlier, complaints were made that the information provided by personnel departments was not sufficiently 'hard', that it lacked quantification, that no very useful data base had ever been assembled, and so on. There seemed to be three basic reasons for this deficiency. First, many personnel specialists believed that the nature of the data they were dealing with did not lend itself to quantification, that too many intangibles and issues of judgement were involved, that the complexities of human behaviour would be over-simplified and mis-represented in bald statistics and that such statistics might therefore be misleading if used as a basis for decision-making. Second, this belief tended to reflect a lack of expertise in the systematic diagnosis of problem areas, so that, given the absence of analytic modelling of these areas, no frame-work could be readily evolved to direct data collection and analysis as a first step to problem solution. Third, a major stimulus to this approach to personnel management activities is a recognition of the need for at least medium-term planning of the acquisition, maintenance, and development of employees, but, as was discussed earlier, this recognition was by no means universally held, generally owing to misconceptions about the nature of planning itself. Thus, personnel managers often questioned the value of manpower planning in rapidly changing product and labour market environments, without realizing that techniques existed to model the range and degree of change that might be experienced in market environments, along with the manpower strategies appropriate to anti-cipated alternative outcomes.

However, as human resources become more costly, there should be less tolerance of this *ad hoc*, unsystematic approach and more support and recognition given to the development of expertise in a range of technical areas where quantitative methods may be combined with the application of social and management science knowledge. This is particularly notable in areas in which employees are seen as involving direct costs, i.e., wage and salary policy and manpower acquisition and development. For example there is growing interest in and development of techniques of job evaluation, such as the time span of discretion method (Jaques, 1961, 1964; Fox, 1966b), the decision-band method (Paterson 1972), the Hay–MSL method (Paterson, 1972; Van Horn, 1972; Younger, 1975); and the castellion method (Paterson, 1972), for application to both wage and salary systems, together with the increased use of salary progression curves (McBeath and Rands, 1969; McBeath, 1969; Bowley, 1971; Rock, 1972). Also, there is the more general use of systematic recruitment and selection procedures, within a context of a manpower plan that does not fight shy of the use of the statistical modelling techniques involved in the development of renewal models, transition or Markov chain models or stationary models (Bartholomew, 1967; Bartholomew and Morris, 1971; Smith, 1971; Stainer, 1971; Keeny, 1973; Bartholomew, 1976).

Attempts to develop a more systematic approach in one area (e.g., job evaluation in relation to the design of the salary systems) tend to highlight the need to do the same in a related area (e.g., training), a spill-over well illustrated in Thomason's model of elements and their inter-relationships in a manpower planning programme (see Fig. 4.1).

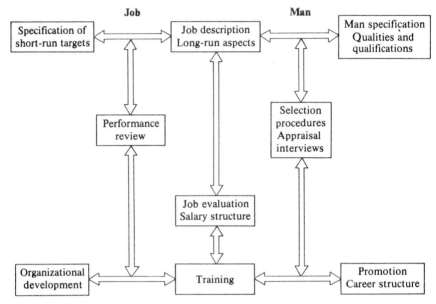

Figure 4.1. Elements and their inter-relationships in a manpower planning programme. (From Thomason (1975), Fig. 5, page 294.)

Generally speaking then, this approach of systematizing human resources management, on the basis of social and management science knowledge, tends to emphasize the personnel professional's value in improving the quality of managerial control.

If the personnel specialist engages in conformist innovation, he is using power based on expertise to improve the position of his department. Expertise can, of course, be a source of professional power, when it is used to legitimize an occupation's acquisition and retention of an institutionalized professional status, as discussed earlier, but in these circumstances it comes closer to the basis of scientific authority, as understood in Hughes's distinction. That is, the personnel specialist grounds his activities in specialist technical competence, such as quantitative method, the value of which is clearly acknowledged by his colleagues (other managers). Furthermore, his choice of where, in what way, and to what ends he will employ his technical expertise is determined by financial criteria in line with the organization's dominant value system, rather than in an attempt to alter it. In other words, the personnel specialist attempts to increase his power by integrating himself more closely (by increasing his 'centrality' and 'non-substitutability') in the main stream of organizational activities and values.

In these circumstances, becoming a 'professional' personnel manager will be seen as chiefly involving the acquisition of certain skills that derive from a body of knowledge and are largely obtained through education and training. The skills that are required will be those that can be demonstrated as relevant and useful in performing the personnel function in the manner described above. The desire to restrict entry into the personnel 'profession' to those with, say, IPM qualifications and membership, is likely to develop, as the specialists will argue that their status and credibility will be undermined if those without proof of expertise in this 'specialist' area are employed. This being so, the 'trait' model of professionalism is likely to be that chosen and used by 'conformist innovators'.

However, many personnel specialists would reject the value implications of this approach (which we would term 'bureaucratic/utilitarian') and opt for what may be called *'deviant' innovation*.

'Deviant' innovation

Whereas the 'conformist' innovator goes along with the existing organizational ends and 'adjusts' his means to achieve them, rather than making his activities conform to the dominant values about what constitutes organizational success, the 'deviant innovator' *attempts to change this means/ends relationship by gaining acceptance for a different set of criteria for the evaluation of organizational success and his contribution to it* (cf., Merton, 1957). For instance, he may argue that, contrary to the prevailing managerial view, organizational *efficiency* and *effectiveness* are not necessarily synonymous. Whereas organizational efficiency may be regarded as the ratio of energic output to energic input (Katz and Kahn, 1966; Becker and Neuhauser, 1975) and, hence, for practical purposes, expressed adequately if not optimally in financial terms, organizational effectiveness, defined as the maximization of return to the organization by all means and thus involving some assumptions with respect to the frames of reference employed, is a much broader concept. For example, if organizational effectiveness is considered from the point of view of one of its members, it may be defined as that which offers the greatest aggregate return to that member in terms of all forms of job satisfaction including such intangibles as opportunities for self-actualization, and so on. In these circumstances, the criteria appropriate to measure organizational effectiveness must necessarily involve values other than, and supplementary to, those used in the measurement of efficiency alone. Thus, it has been argued by at least one commentator that a major responsibility of the personnel specialist should be to act as 'the interpreter and advocate' of society to the corporation, to make his organization aware that its dominant values are not necessarily the same as, or in the long-term interests of, society as a whole.

> Perhaps it is too much to ask that he (the personnel specialist) become a partisan of the big society, but if not, then he must at least subdue his ardor for classic business ideology sufficiently so that he can remain cognizant of the trends of the twentieth century without anguish or anger. He must be able to recognize what is happening outside the corporate walls, to consider it coolly, to interpret it, and to transmit an undistorted picture to those in charge of his company. His mission must also be to try to make them understand the picture—not necessarily to approve of it but to understand it realistically. And he must do all of these things—functions very different from the responsibilities of his fellow managers who are profit oriented—without shame or apology. (Herman, 1968, page 309.)

If the personnel specialist takes this standpoint, not only does he argue the case for the consideration of a supplementary, if not at times incompatible set of values, but he introduces an external reference group for the evaluation of his own and the organization's activities.[10]

If he can gain real acceptance for these non-financial values and, with it, the admission of an external reference group, and if he has expertise in these newly valued areas, the personnel specialist is better placed to base his role and relationships and thus his authority on a 'professional' rather than purely managerial footing. In other words, he (*not* the consumers of his service) has the right to define their 'personnel' needs and how these needs should be met, according to his own 'professional' expertise and beliefs as to what is appropriate in the light of the 'new' values the organization has adopted. Thus, those using the services he offers become clients rather than customers as they accept the specialist's definition of what activities he should provide rather than asserting their right to specify or choose. Further, they may accept his right to, and authority in, this initiating role on the basis of his reputation among his peers (i.e., other specialists in his field) and suspend their own claim to judge his performance and the validity of his activities on the basis of their own ideas as to what is appropriate. If the personnel specialist is able to restructure his relationships with other managerial groups in this fashion, he has in fact come close to establishing 'professional' control over his occupation in terms of Johnson's definition.

In practice, of course, few personnel specialists are able to change dominant organizational values to this extent and exert this level of control over their relationships with other groups in the organization. They may, however, be able to persuade other groups of the necessity of deferring to certain humanistic values as a precondition to the achievement of success in terms of the dominant values. Interestingly enough, some movement in this direction occurs when personnel specialists adopt the role of the internal consultant in what might be termed the 'old professional' areas of

[10] Cf., Sayles's comment that 'innovation groups represent the extreme of professionalization in the organization, insofar as their standards of performance can be set by outside reference groups' (see Sayles, 1964, page 109).

clinical and legal expertise. Thus, in his attempts to gain acceptance of policies based on humanistic rather than on unequivocally utilitarian values, the 'deviant innovator' has to some extent been legitimized by sources of authority outside his immediate organization: namely by the 'Organizational Development' movement and by legislation.

Organizational development. Basically, the values, processes, and techniques that cluster under the umbrella-like label of OD are a response to the problem of organizational adaptation to rapid rates of change, both in terms of technologies and social values (Beer, 1972; Toffler, 1970). The changes discussed at the beginning of this chapter are themselves examples of this phenomenon. While OD may be viewed as a system of three related elements, viz., values, process (i.e., data gathering, organizational diagnosis, and action intervention, such as sensitivity training or team building), and technology (i.e., techniques and methods emerging primarily from the behavioural sciences), it is first and foremost its value base that provides support and rationale for the 'deviant innovator'. Margulies and Raia have summarized these values as follows:

1. Providing opportunities for people to function as human beings rather than as resources in the productive process.[11]
2. Providing opportunities for each organization member, as well as for the organization itself, to develop to his full potential.
3. Seeking to increase the effectiveness of the organization in terms of *all* its goals.
4. Attempting to create an environment in which it is possible to find exacting and challenging work.
5. Providing opportunities for people in organizations to influence the way in which they relate to work, the organization, and the environment.
6. Treating each human being as a person with a complex set of needs, *all* of which are important in his work and in his life (1972, page 3).

It is these humanistic values, it is argued, that by placing organizational relationships on a new basis of openness, trust, and collaboration,[12] create

[11] If the personnel specialist attempts this approach with its emphasis on altruistic rather than utilitarian values, he is essentially introducing a new definition of what the personnel *function* should be, as his orientation moves from regarding employees as implements of production—human resources—to ends in themselves, or as one writer has put it 'resourceful humans,' (see Morris and Burgoyne, 1973).

[12] See, for example, Tannenbaum and Davis's (1969) view of the organizational implications of the value position involved in OD. They suggest that the values of OD involve a movement:
—Away from a view of man as essentially bad toward a view of him as basically good.
—Away from avoidance or negative evaluation of individuals toward confirming them as human beings.
—Away from a view of individuals as fixed toward seeing them as being in process.
—Away from resisting and fearing individual differences toward accepting and utilizing them.
—Away from maskmanship and game-playing toward authentic behavior.
—Away from use of status for maintaining power and personal prestige toward use of status for organizationally relevant purposes.

Cont. next page

a climate conducive to absorbing and even welcoming the challenge of innovation. Thus, OD, in spite of its insistence on overtly non-financial success criteria (such as measures of personal growth and of increased openness in organizational problem-solving and decision-making), can ultimately be reconciled with conventional organizational goals (and success criteria), if it is accepted that adaptation to all forms of environment change is essential to organizational survival and growth, and that the ability to do this is promoted by OD strategies. Implicit in many OD programmes is the view that, given changing social values, the achievement of efficiency both will depend on, and be a tangible outcome of, an effective organization (in the OD sense), even if this prohibits its maximization. Thus, whereas in the 'conformist innovator's' view effectiveness is a by-product or a luxury that may be developed on the basis of the efficiency, in the 'deviant innovator's' view, not only is it of value in itself, but provides the basis for achieving efficiency in the long term. This difference in emphasis may be characterized as the contrast between those who prefer to see organizational behaviour in terms of models of control and those who prefer motivation models. (Cf., Lupton and Gowler, 1972.)

If the 'deviant innovator' with these arguments can win the acceptance of the value of an OD strategy, with its various success criteria, he can then develop a basis of support through the introduction of an external reference group, the OD consultants[13] (a necessary component of a 'proper' OD programme) for a new assessment of relationships and activities, including his own, throughout the organization (Margulies and Raia, 1972). In the course of the OD programme, he may also be able to develop

---

[13] It should be noted, however, that some personnel specialists, often those seeking legitimacy through the 'conformist innovator' approach, find OD consultants a challenge and potential threat to their own position and programmes, in the competition for material and ideological resources. The need for co-ordination of their not *necessarily* incompatible efforts is clearly pointed out by French (1969).

Footnote 12 (cont.)

—Away from distrusting people toward trusting them.
—Away from avoiding facing others with relevant data toward making appropriate confrontation.
—Away from avoidance of risk-taking towards willingness to risk.
—Away from a view of process work as being unproductive effort toward seeing it as essential to effective task accomplishment.
—Away from a primary emphasis on competition toward a much greater emphasis on collaboration.

See also French's (1969) similar list of OD objectives:

1. To increase the level of trust and support among organizational members.
2. To increase the incidence of confrontation of organizational problems, both within groups and among groups in contrast to 'sweeping problems under the rug'.
3. To create an environment in which authority of assigned role is augmented by authority based on knowledge and skill.
4. To increase the openness of communications laterally, vertically, and diagonally.
5. To increase the level of personal enthusiasm and satisfaction in the organization.
6. To find synergistic solutions to problems with greater frequency.
7. To increase the level of self and group responsibility in planning and implementation.

an expertise in OD processes and technology (e.g., in organizational diagnosis, in the theory of group dynamics, in activities such as team building and sensitivity training) and in this way augment his authority by increasing his identification with a 'professional' group, whose expertise is based on 'external' behavioural science knowledge, not readily available in the client organization. In time, he may inherit the external consultants' mantle, for having acted as catalysts to change, their role is to encourage the development of a self-sustaining system internal to the organization and to discourage the emergence of a dependency relationship between themselves and the client organization.

With the departure of the external consultants, and their 'professional' support, the 'deviant innovator' is unlikely to be able to maintain his authority on the 'professional' basis (i.e., professional peer group evaluation) that they enjoyed. Instead, as a prophet in his own country while drawing some support from his connection with the external consultants,[14] his credibility may come to rest on his ability to show a clear relationship between the increased organizational effectiveness (in OD terms) that he has achieved, and organizational efficiency (measured in financial terms). In other words, it may rest on the evaluation of his clients (a non-professional, bureaucratic evaluation). However, a halfway house may be reached if these consumers of his services are persuaded of the specialist's own definition of what constitutes a success in this area. In these circumstances, he may be evaluated in terms of the nature and quality of his relationships with his clients as ends in themselves. For example, in terms of the new perspectives he can bring to analysing a problem, or the supportiveness of his advice, or his independence, or his qualities as a mediator between different interest groups and as a facilitator for others' development, rather than on the quantifiable outcomes of activities moulded directly round the dominant, if probably short-term, financial values.

Legislation. As indicated earlier in this chapter, organizations, in the last decade, have been inundated by a spate of legislation which shows no sign of abating. Indeed, EEC membership and pressures for legislative action on industrial democracy are likely to effect an acceleration. Basically, it has aimed at securing various rights for employees (e.g., the Contract of Employment Acts, the Employment Protection Act), quite apart from that imposing obligations on employer and employee alike (e.g., Statutory Incomes Policy) in the interest of the country at large. In particular, the effect of the former, in conjunction with increasingly militant collective action, including collective bargaining, has been to challenge traditional managerial prerogatives and to alter permanently the relationship between employer and employee. As Thomason puts it:

---

[14] *If* they were deemed successful, against whatever criteria they were evaluated, by the power-holders and/or opinion leaders within the organization (cf., Warmington, 1975; also Foulkes and Morgan, 1977).

Instead of having privileges at the grace and favour of the employer, perhaps upheld in power bargaining by the workers' associations, the worker has now either established by his collective power, or been granted through legislation, that these privileges are his by right (1975, page 25).

Thomason goes on to point out that the imposition of standards from outside the organization (in the form of statutory duties), combined with the fact that legislation has given employees legally enforceable rights, which are therefore capable of being expressed as a financial cost to the employer, has two major implications for the personnel manager. First, it may allow him 'a more independent role' within the organization, an idea similar to Herman's view of the personnel specialist representing the interests of the wider society to the rest of management. Second, it may 'serve to shift the balance of criteria of judgement of success' (1975, page 429) away from purely 'efficiency criteria' towards a consideration of those concerned with 'social costs and benefits' (page 427) both within and outside the immediate organization, with the development of a 'corporate conscience' (page 430).

Moreover, these implications of existing legislation are likely to be further reinforced by pending company law reform (Wedderburn, 1965; Gower, 1969; Fogarty, 1975; Epstein, 1977). Proposals in the 1973 White Paper on Company Law Reform, echoed by the CBI (1973) report, admit that the relevant constituencies in corporate administration should extend beyond shareholders, directors, and management, to employees, consumers, and the public at large. In particular, it has been argued (White Paper, 1973) that disclosure of information on such matters as the performance of the company with regard to the health and safety of its employees, the conduct of industrial relations, and the number of consumer complaints and how they were dealt with, would 'give share-holders and the public the chance to judge companies' behaviour by social as well as financial criteria' (page 7, para 12). Also, the impetus for company law reform of this nature is likely to obtain added reinforcement from existing proposals for the harmonization of EEC companies law (Commission of the European Communities, 1975).

Legislation may then act as a powerful support to the personnel specialist who seeks to increase his authority through 'deviant innovation'. Because legislation has placed, and will continue to place, restrictions on an organization's freedom to pursue its dominant success criteria, even to the point of having to redefine some of them, when the personnel specialist adopts the role of the independent legal expert in relation to these issues, his advice is backed by the authority of the law and as such compels attention on the part of his colleagues/clients.

Oscillations

Neither of these attempts to gain 'professional' authority is, by itself, fully viable in all circumstances. However much the 'conformist innovator' attempts to use 'professional' expertise to demonstrate personnel's contribution to organizational success in tangible financial terms, the fact remains that the contribution *is* an indirect one, and that many of the developmental activities, especially, are extremely difficult to evaluate in this way. At best the approach can have a depressingly negative air, for as Herman writes:

> The trouble is . . . that for the most part it is very difficult even to pretend to measure the dollar value of what personnel work is concerned with. As a result, many times the personnel department has to fall back on 'might-have-been' and 'might-have-done' estimates—what the union might have done (and its cost) if the negotiations team had not done such a masterful job of negotiating the contract, for instance, or on the other hand, what might have been the improvement in production if the personnel department had been allowed to put its new communications program into effect (1968, pages 34–35).

On the other hand, attempts by the 'deviant innovator' to gain acceptance of a new set of organizational ends that should not necessarily be evaluated in financial terms and, at the same time, to convince other managerial groups that the achievement of these 'debatable' objectives requires a realignment of traditional relationships and sources of authority, is likely to provoke resistance on the part of those who accept existing dominant organizational values.

Elsewhere, it has been suggested (Legge and Exley, 1975) that in practice, personnel specialists will tend to oscillate between these two paths to professional authority, depending on the stage that they have reached in their career and on the organizational environment in which they are placed (see fig. 4.2). In terms of career development, it is likely that the more junior personnel specialist will tend towards the strategy of conformist innovation, if against his inclination, for several reasons. First, he is still 'working his passage' and hence will probably wish to 'fit in' and conform to the dominant values of his superiors which, on balance, are likely to be financial. Second, conformist innovation can be applied directly to routine company wide personnel programmes (e.g., performance appraisal, salary systems, recruitment and selection in the context of manpower planning) without necessarily involving the initiation of radical programmes involving new values and unfamiliar objectives, as might an OD programme, for example. Hence, it is often easier to get started on conformist innovation from a low power base than it is to undertake deviant innovation. In contrast, the 'deviant innovator' may have to confront the value systems of colleagues and superordinates and engage in a long process of marketing his ideas before they can be expressed in a coherent set of activities, and then perhaps implemented in only one 'experimental' site, rather than throughout the organization. In these circumstances, it is to his advantage if he has already gained respect and authority from the successful performance of conformist innovation type activities, so that he can speak as one who has proved himself within the

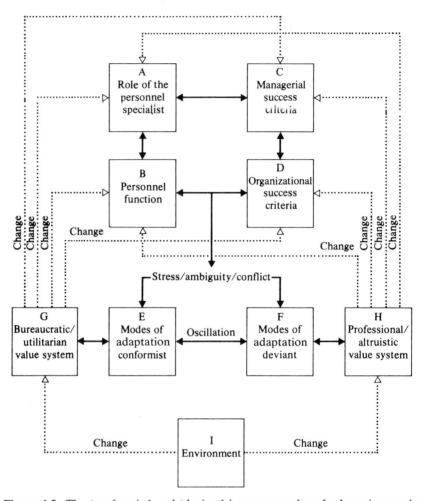

Figure 4.2. The 'conformist' and 'deviant' innovator styles of adaptation to the dilemmas confronting personnel specialists (From Legge and Exley (1975), Fig. 1, page 64).

value system that he wishes to modify, rather than appear to argue from a position of failure. A corollary to this is that the 'deviant innovator' stands more chance of success in this strategy if he has already achieved a relatively senior position within his department so that he has at least direct access to the power holders within the organization. This is essential, as activities such as an OD programme require support from the top in both financial terms (e.g., for the high fees of external consultants) and ideological commitment if any real change of organizational climate is to be achieved (Margulies and Raia, 1972; Klein, 1976).

The organizational environment, particularly in terms of its economic viability, is also likely to influence which strategy stands the best chance of success. It is noticeable that in deflationary situations, when organizations may be suffering from liquidity and related problems, the urge to 'cut back' is reflected in a close attention to financial considerations. When this occurs, the strategy adopted by the 'conformist innovator' is likely to prove far more acceptable than that adopted by the 'deviant innovator'. Indeed, when adverse economic circumstances exist, the proposal that an organization adopt success criteria which, though involving the generation of costs, cannot be shown to produce immediately quantifiable financial benefits, is likely to be greeted as an unjustifiable luxury.

Alternatively, in periods of economic boom, the climate for experimentation of all kinds is likely to be more favourable than at other times, as sufficient resources and organizational slack are being generated to fund it. Further, in such circumstances, the prevailing atmosphere of confidence may stimulate senior management's interest in the more 'positive', growth-oriented aspects of corporate strategy (such as ways to improve motivation and, hopefully, productivity, market share and profits) and relieve its pre-occupation with negative, survival-oriented activity, such as cost control. 'Deviant innovators' generally require such a climate in which to develop. For it is in these circumstances that the organization may feel free to experiment with new objectives or with new ways of achieving old ones. Furthermore, while the pressures arising from adverse economic conditions are likely to reinforce bureaucratic, hierarchically based patterns of authority, the buffers created by a more favourable economic environment may allow the development of the relationships and patterns of authority appropriate to the achievement of new organizational success criteria.

However, an exception to this general pattern is likely to exist in situations of extreme economic or social difficulty (such as impending bankruptcy or an anarchic industrial relations record). In this circumstance, it has been suggested (Greiner, 1967; Bailey, 1973) that an enforced questioning of dominant values, coupled with a willingness to 'try anything once' to stave off total disaster, may actually lend support to the strategies of the 'deviant innovator'. It may be remembered that early, and the most successful adoptions of the then-revolutionary Scanlon plan, were made by companies facing bankruptcy—not to mention the present rash of workers' co-operatives.

While environmental and organizational change encourages these oscillatory tendencies, it can give rise to serious problems of phasing. Given that time lags are involved in the design, generation of resources, and implementation of any strategy, what may have appeared an environmentally appropriate approach at the date of conception, may, by the time of implementation, have become singularly inappropriate. Given the inherently long-term orientation of much of the work of the 'deviant innovator', this problem is one that is likely to present particular difficulties to his approach. Hence, it must be borne in mind that the personnel specialist, adopting this approach needs to maintain a continuing set of steady-state activities, competently exercised, if not in an aggressively 'conformist innovator' style that may prove incompatible with his longer term objectives, as a base from which to develop, when circumstances are favourable.

Although it is considered that the ability to undertake conformist or deviant innovation is either impeded or facilitated by circumstances, in the manner suggested above, this is not to say that those which *facilitate* a particular strategy are those, in terms of organizational growth and survival, that are most *appropriate* to it. This may or may not be the case and will be dealt with in the concluding chapter. But before this question is tackled, it is necessary to consider a third way in which the personnel specialist might seek to increase his credibility with other managerial groups, an approach which, while still a form of professionalism, takes a more pragmatic approach to the task of personnel management. That is, the approach of the problem-solver, operating on the basis of contingency theory. It is this approach that is considered in the following chapter.

5. A contingent approach to personnel management: I

In the previous chapter, it was suggested that personnel specialists who seek to increase their credibility and authority tend to oscillate between two modes of adaptation to the situations they confront, namely 'conformist' and 'deviant' innovation. Although these modes of adaptation may be represented as roles in themselves, they may also be regarded as two different ways or styles of performing the same role, that of the problem-solver.

The personnel specialist as problem-solver

The role of the personnel specialist as problem-solver has been recognized by so many commentators (e.g., Strauss and Sayles, 1960; Lupton, 1964; Crichton, 1968; Miner and Miner, 1973; Glueck, 1974) that it would now seem to be the prevailing model, not only of the direction personnel management as a specialist activity should take, but the approach appropriate to other management groups when carrying out their part of the personnel function (Margerison, 1976b). Although criticisms have already been made of how inadequately this approach is dealt with by many of the textbooks, nevertheless, in itself, it has much to recommend it.

The role of the personnel specialist as problem-solver has been seen to involve three main activities. First, he needs to *conceptualize* the nature of problem(s) he has to deal with. McFarland (1968, page 36) has characterized this activity as involving the following elements: an awareness of an area of difficulty and/or holding the opportunity of improvement; a careful search for the basic causes of the difficulty/opportunity; knowledge of related or contributing patterns of causes and conditions; information on the costs and penalties of alternative actions, estimates of probable consequences of available practicable alternatives. In other words, *conceptualizing* the nature of a problem goes in hand in hand with *diagnostic* activities and involves an iterative process. It is on the outcome of this formulation and analysis of the problem that specific *strategies* for its solution are determined and courses of action implemented. So important a part are the diagnostic activities seen to play in this process of problem solution that some commentators have characterized the role in these terms. Hence, Lupton (1964) speaks of the need for personnel special to become 'organizational diagnosticians' if they wish to gain recognition having an essential contribution to make to organizational policy-ma while Glueck states 'the ideal administrator has as his model the physician (1974, page 6). It is interesting, in the light of earlier comments on professionalism, that it is to the role of the doctor, that archetype of a professional, that Glueck turns to provide an example of an occupation founded on a diagnostic approach. This analogy is additionally appropriate as medical problem-solving involves not only diagnosing and managing existing dysfunctions in the patient, but emphasizing the need for continuing preventative work as the best way to control and, hopefully, eradicate such dysfunctions. Similarly, while concerned with the efficient diagnosis and handling of problems already existing in the organization, often the result of inadequate or inappropriate organizational design in the past, the organizational diagnostician's chief concern is to eliminate the need for this day-to-day problem-solving by better organizational design in the first place. Hence, strategy formulation for the personnel specialist as problem solver is at two levels: coping with the symptoms of existing organizational dysfunctions, and designing systems that will prevent the occurrence of such problems in the future.

For 'organizational diagnosis' to take place at all, it is obvious that the practitioner must have some body of knowledge or frame of reference on which to base his diagnosis. Again, most commentators are agreed what this should be: knowledge must be based on 'behavioral science research' (Miner and Miner, 1973, page vi), or as Lupton (1964) puts it 'personnel management must increasingly become the application of behavioural sciences to the problems of the structure and functioning of industrial and commercial organizations'. Yet the question still remains, in terms of what theoretical *orientation* should the findings of social science itself be utilized, what meta theory should direct the choice and application of particular social science concepts to different problem areas?

Many commentators (Lupton, 1964, 1970, 1975b; Miner and Miner, 1973; Glueck, 1974) have either explicitly or implicitly applied social science to organizational problem-solving within the framework of *contingency theory* (cf., Gordon *et al.*, 1974). However, their approaches vary somewhat, due to their different understandings as to what the theory involves. For 'the contingent approach' can be understood in both *positive/descriptive* and *normative* terms, although a shift of meaning occurs. In its positive sense, as used for example by Lawrence and Lorsch (1967a), contingency theory rests on the assumption that because 'organizational variables are in a complex inter-relationship with one another and with conditions in the environment ... it is possible to understand the differences in the internal states and processes of organizations on the basis of differences in the external environment'. In other words, contingency theory in its positive sense just makes the theoretical point that it is 'contingencies' in an organization's environment that, acting as both constraints and opportunities, influence the organization's internal structures and processes. In using this approach, contingency theorists generally have employed socio-technical systems analysis[1] allied to a structural-functionalist[2] view of organization to explain why and in what ways situations can be characterized as differing from each other. From this purely descriptive position, the implication was drawn that because situations differed, there can be no one 'best' way to organize, or tackle a problem (such as management appraisal or the design of any control system), but rather that the appropriate solution *depends* on the specific nature of relevant organizational and environmental characteristics and their inter-relationships. Hence, methods of organization or control systems (e.g., payment systems, the division of labour, or even managerial style) which were previously regarded simply as independent variables affecting a situation (e.g., the effect of a payment system on labour turnover), now could be seen as variables dependent on the context in which they were applied (e.g., the effect of labour turnover on a payment system). From this half-way house of examining the implications of this theory for practice, it was a short step to arriving at a fully-fledged normative stance. For the appropriateness of any strategy, in an exercise of organizational design, will depend not only on the nature of organizational and environmental characteristics and their inter-relationships, but on the *objectives* sought by the exercise. (Indeed, at this point, purely descriptive contingency theory may be lost sight of as in practice these objectives are likely to determine

---

[1] Socio-technical systems analysis rests on two assumptions: (a) that the social relations that develop in a work place are related to the technological character of the work and that (b) the variables involved will be related to each other causally in a complex, interactive way, and that is is the *relations* between variables which are of most significance in formulating any explanation of the characteristics and the behaviour of a particular system of organization (for further discussion of systems theory see Trist *et al.*, 1963; Emery, 1969).

[2] Structural-functionalism is that approach to organizational analysis that, placing emphasis on the delineation of major structural-variables and their inter-relationships, (a) views the organization as a system with a need to survive and adjust to its environment, and, consequently, (b) views activities or conditions within the organization as contributing functionally to its maintenance or development, or dysfunctionally to its disintegration and ineffectiveness.

which contextual variables and their inter-relationships are selected as relevant in the diagnostic stage of problem-solving, and which are ignored, a problem with all contextual positions.)

But it is this aspect of contingency theory that suggests its potential utility and appeal to the conformist and deviant innovator alike. The method does not predetermine the objectives to be sought, it only suggests that they feature prominently in problem-solving/organizational design activities, as a crucial aspect of organizational context. It can therefore be employed flexibly to design strategies to achieve either existing or new organizational success criteria. Hence, as with the role of problem-solver itself, this approach to the activities involved is equally applicable to both types of innovator.

Whether the commentator leans towards a positive/descriptive or normative use of contingency theory will influence how he tackles organizational problem-solving. If, like Miner and Miner (1973, page 46), he emphasizes its normative use, more attention is likely to be directed to strategy formulation than to the modelling of the *inter-relationships* of organizational and environmental variables on which this formulation ultimately depends. Rather than first developing a *dynamic model* of these processes, as contingency theory in its positive sense demands, a checklist approach to organizational context is often employed, whereby 'key' organizational and environmental variables are identified, but their inter-relationships treated sketchily and, more importantly, the *processes* of their interaction ignored.[3] Because of this, the resulting strategy formulation may be impaired, although it may still be an improvement on the unrealistic approaches that it is beginning to supersede.

Alternatively, to concentrate on using contingency theory descriptively may lead to its potential employment as a management tool being neglected, overshadowed (and possibly devalued in managerial circles) by its use in increasingly complex academic analysis and model-building, as a tool for research alone.

Ideally, of course, the two approaches are best combined, so that contingency theory is used normatively, but only after descriptive analysis and model-building based on empirical research. In this way, the emphasis is evenly balanced: the need for modelling organizational and environmental context in a way that takes account of complex interaction and feedback is seen as a necessary first step towards a more credible approach to organization design and, hence, in the long term, more successful problem prevention as well as solution.

---

[3] See, for example, the checklist approach of Miner and Miner (1973, chapters 4 and 5) and that of Glueck (1974, pages 7–10, chapter 3). Note that even where a *model* of the organizational and environmental variables relevant to personnel management decision-making is presented (e.g., Glueck, Fig. I.I), although some relationships are sketched out the processes of interaction and feedback are largely ignored.

This has been the approach employed by commentators such as Lupton and Gowler (1969), Mumford (1972a, 1972b, 1976), Vroom and Yetton (1973), in tackling such diverse areas in personnel management as wage payment systems design and management, job design and the development of managerial styles appropriate to different categories of decision-making. Hence, in the next section, by way of example, their approaches to these issues are used to illustrate the five basic steps in applying contingency theory to managerial problem-solving.

A contingent approach to managerial problem-solving

The logic of a contingent approach, combining both the descriptive and normative aspects of the theory, demands the application of several common procedures. These are:

1. An objective-setting exercise, based on a diagnosis of what specific objectives are appropriate to the organizational context involved.
2. An analytical classification of the alternatives (whether payment systems or managerial styles or different approaches to re-organizing work) that are the subject of the design exercise.
3. An analysis, preferably involving the construction of a dynamic processual model, of the context in which such an alternative is to apply.
4. The selection of one of the alternatives on the basis that it 'fits' the context in which it is to operate in such a way as to facilitate the achievement of the specified objectives.
5. A recognition of the need to evaluate systematically not only the basis for selecting a specific alternative in the first instance, but its degree of success following implementation.

While (1) and (5) rest on the normative use of contingency theory, (2) and (3) involve diagnostic analysis from a more descriptive standpoint, while (4) spans both approaches.

Each of these five steps may now be illustrated with reference to the work cited above.

Objective setting. First, those taking a contingent approach to managerial problem-solving should be clear about

(a) *why* they need to make fully explicit their objectives in such exercises, and
(b) *how* and on what basis such objectives should be formulated.

Lupton and Gowler (1969) discuss the first question in relation to the designing of wage payment systems. Clarifying objectives has a dual function: it both enables managers to take their own values and objectives into account in the design process, and it encourages them to evaluate the consequences of holding them in their current or future situation. For example, it is not enough for management (and those others involved) just to decide what objectives an existing or future wage payment system should achieve (i.e., what a payment system *should* do), preferably in the light of various organizational success criteria; management must also be able to analyse what functions[4] (and dysfunctions) their existing wage payment systems perform for the bargaining units in which they operate, and for the organization as a whole. In other words, *how does an existing* payment system operate? (irrespective of *how* it *should*); what purposes is it perceived to serve by management and workers, in operating in the way it does?; what problems is it perceived to give rise to, and why? The question of what functions existing payment systems (or modes of decision-making, or pattern of working arrangements) serve is crucial. For, if their unintended beneficial consequences are not noted, they may be modified or replaced without regard for these 'latent functions'.

The question of how objectives should then be formulated raises other issues. Obviously, at the most general level, the objective of any managerial attempt at organizational problem-solving could be expressed in terms of increasing 'organizational effectiveness'. Yet the way 'effectiveness' is to be defined and measured has to be made explicit (what success criteria are to be used?) and in doing so, this general goal or value has to be translated into more specific and measurable objectives whose achievement may comprise a means to this end. Thus, Vroom and Yetton discuss organizational effectiveness in terms of the immediate objective of improving the quality of managerial decision-making, which in turn is defined and measured in terms of managers' ability to achieve the operational goals (e.g., reducing costs by 30 per cent, re-organizing to adapt to a cut in manpower while maintaining volume) explicit in the statements of the problems to which their decision-making is addressed.

A good example of how an objective-selecting exercise might be carried out is the method employed by Mumford in selecting objectives for a job redesign programme. First, she makes explicit her value position that job redesign may increase organizational effectiveness through achieving greater employee job satisfaction and organizational efficiency, by obtaining an improved match between what an organization requires of its employees and what they require of it, between what the employee is seeking from the firm and what he is receiving. The matches and mismatches between organizational and employee needs (and between his needs and what he receives from the organization) may then be examined by viewing work relationships as a series of five contracts between

---

[4] To prevent confusion, following the discussion about the meaning of the term 'function' in chapter 2, here it may be defined as the objective consequences of the existence and/or action of persons or things for some system, especially for the integration and adaptation of that system. 'Dysfunction' may be defined as a consequence that is considered to detract from the integration, effectiveness etc., of the system in which it occurs. 'Latent function' is defined as positive consequences for a system which are neither intended nor anticipated (see Merton, 1957).

	The firm	The employee
The KNOWLEDGE contract	Needs a certain level of skill and knowledge in its employees if it is to function efficiently	Wishes the skills and knowledge he brings with him to be used and developed
The PSYCHOLOG-ICAL contract	Needs employees who are *motivated* to look after its interests	Seeks to further interests private to himself, e.g., to secure: Achievement Recognition Responsibility Status
The EFFICIENCY/ REWARDS contract	Needs to implement generalized output and quality standards and reward systems	Seeks a personal, equitable effort-reward bargain, and controls, including supervisory ones, which he perceives as acceptable
The ETHICAL (social value) contract	Needs employees who will accept the firm's ethos and values	Seeks to work for an employer whose values do not contravene his own
The TASK STRUCTURE contract	Needs employees who will accept technical and other constraints which produce task specificity or task differentiation	Seeks a set of tasks which meets his requirements for task differentiation, e.g., which incorporate variety, interests, targets, feedback, task identity and autonomy

Figure 5.1. The five contracts (after Mumford, 1972a)

management and employees. These contracts are set out in Fig. 5.1 above,[5] If an employee's needs in these five areas are met, then he is hypothesized to have high job satisfaction; if, at the same time those of the employing organization are also met, then a 'mutually beneficial environment for both sets of interested parties will have been achieved' (Mumford, 1972a, page

[5] The meta theory from which these five contracts are derived is the Parsonian model of pattern variables. Parsons saw individuals as evaluating all situations in terms of (a) what they expect to happen, and (b) what they can influence in the situation to give themselves a choice of outcome. Thus, individuals are presented with a series of choices which must be made before a situation can become meaningful and specific action be taken. These choices can be categorized into five dichotomies or 'Pattern variables' (i.e., the tendency to choose one pattern rather than another in a particular type of situation). This choice is made in terms of personal expectations, needs and objectives, and covers the following alternatives (as termed by Parsons) between

Affectivity and affectivity neutrality
Self-orientation and collectivity orientation
Universalism and particularism
Ascription and achievement
Speciality and diffusiveness

Cont. next page

51). Using a questionnaire[6] based on these five contracts, employees' job satisfaction needs can be diagnosed. At the same time, to arrive at efficiency needs from the organization's point of view, analysis needs to be undertaken to identify aspects of work where high performance is not being achieved. The method Mumford employs is that of 'variance analysis', an approach that has been developed by Davis (see Taylor, 1975). This involves a detailed examination of all the different operations a department or work group undertakes, with the intention of discovering where and why 'variance' (i.e., a deviation from some desired operating standard or specification, involving system weaknesses associated with the organization of work operations) tends to arise. Using this method involves making a precise description of each variance and answering the following questions (I quote):

1. Where in the work process does the variance occur?
2. Where is it first observed?
3. Where is it controlled (corrected)?
4. By whom?
5. What tasks does he have to do to correct it?
6. What information does he get and from what source to enable him to carry out these correction activities? (Mumford, 1976, page 35).

The diagnostic information obtained in the first stage of this job design process may now be used to guide a detailed objective-setting exercise. If, for example (as Mumford points out), employees complain that the existing form of work organization does not enable them to fully utilize or develop their existing skills and knowledge, then improved opportunities in this area can be made a precise objective for the new work system. Equally, from the identification of areas of variances (and their causes), efficiency objectives can be formulated.

Classification of alternative choices. If management and unions are redesigning a wage payment system, or a set of jobs, or if managements are

[6] The complete questionnaire can be obtained from Enid Mumford, Computer and Work Design Research Unit, Manchester Business School, Booth Street West, Manchester, M15 6PB.

Footnote 5 (cont.)

Mumford redefined these dichotomies into terms more amenable for application to the study of job satisfaction, namely:

Company job requirements—personal job requirements
Company interest—self interest
Uniformity—individuality
Performance—personal quality
Work specificity—work flexibility

It is from these dichotomies, thus based on the Parsonian model, that Mumford derives her five contracts. For further elaboration of the nature of these contracts and their operational definitions, see Mumford (1972a, pages 52–54). For a subsequent critique and development of this model, see Gowler (1974).

considering whether their existing style of tackling decision-making is optimal, obviously they need to know something about the range of payment systems, or about the different ways in which jobs can be structured, or about the alternative managerial styles available to choose from. Thus, the second step in this approach is to classify the alternatives that are the focus of the problem-solving exercise. In order to make clear the basis for differentiation, such classifications ideally should be analytic rather than simply descriptive.

So, for example, Lupton and Gowler (1969) provide a classification of payment systems that rests on their analysis of what, in essence, a payment system is: a set of rules and procedures that relate some kind of reward. In such terms they then identify and define several types of effort and reward. For example, they differentiate between (I quote):

1. *Time* effort: when reward is related solely to the amount of time worked, or even attended, at the place of work.
2. *Energy* effort: when reward is related solely to the rate of working, usually measured by the mount of output against a rating scale.
3. *Competence* effort: when reward is related to past effort, i.e., acquired skills and competences which have present and future use.

Reward, defined as any formally recognized mode of payment takes two forms:

1. It can be *immediate* i.e., it is received within the pay period during which the related effort took place.
2. It can be *deferred*, i.e., it is not received within the pay period in which the related effort occurred.

Lupton and Gowler's next step is to identify several different kinds of effort-reward relationships that the rules and procedures comprising the

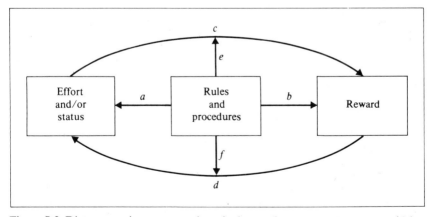

Figure 5.2. Diagrammatic representation of salary and wage payment systems (After Lupton and Gowler (1969), Fig. 11)

payment systems embody. Figure 5.2 illustrates the major relationships. It shows that certain rules and procedures are specifically designed to encourage a feedback from reward to effort (arrows f and d). In this case, reward is further described as *reciprocal*. Where the rules and procedures are not designed to promote this feedback (arrows e and c only), reward is classified as *non-reciprocal*.

			Reward		
			Reciprocal		Non-Reciprocal
			Immediate	Deferred	
Effort		Time	T R I	T R D	T N R
	Energy	Individual	E R I (Ind)	E R D (Ind)	E N R (Ind)
		Group	E R I (Group)	E R D (Group)	E N R (Group)
		Competence	C R I	C R D	C N R
		Status	X	X	S N R

Figure 5.3. The logical grid of payment systems (After Lupton and Gowler (1969), Fig. 2)

A 'logical grid' (Fig. 5.3) attempts to represent all possible types of effort, reward, and effort-reward relationships. Lupton and Gowler then suggest these logically derived types of effort-reward relationships are in practice the basis of different elements in the wage packet and thus different types of payment methods. For example:

Incentive bonus schemes are essentially 'energy reciprocal immediate' (ERI) systems.
Schemes based on universal maintenance standards are 'competence reciprocal immediate' (CRI) systems.
'Work simplification' schemes are 'competence reciprocal deferred' (CRD) systems.
Some measured day work schemes are 'energy non-reciprocal' (ENR) systems.
Fixed salaries are 'competence non-reciprocal' (CNR) systems.

Thus, by this method, Lupton and Gowler analyse the range of alternatives that exist and the main differences in design between different payment methods.

Similarly, Mumford has developed a classification of work that derives from a cybernetic model developed by Beer (1970, 1972). This defines work as having five different levels, viz.:

Level 1, the *operating* level, or the non-discretionary tasks which the employee has to undertake in order to make, process or record something.
Level 2, the *anti-oscillation* level, or those tasks which prevent problems/variances occurring and corrects them if they do and which, additionally, allocates resources.
Level 3, the *optimizing* level, or those tasks which are concerned with the co-ordination of work and with ensuring that tasks are integrated and harmonized in pursuit of specified objectives.
Level 4, the *developmental* level, or those tasks concerned with the presently discretionary aspects of work, where a job can be developed by bringing new ideas to bear on it. It covers opportunities to try out new methods or plan new tasks or objectives.
Level 5, the *overall control* level, or those tasks concerned with the total management of the job and the way in which all levels fit together.

Although essentially descriptive, the taxonomy of five alternative managerial styles of decision-making (Fig. 5.4), provided by Vroom and Yetton (1973, Chapters 1 and 2) is derived from an analysis of the special nature of organizational, as opposed to individual, decision-making. That is, it involves social as well as cognitive processes, and it is these social processes (including the designing, regulating, and selecting of social systems that make decisions) that are of most significance in characterizing managerial style. It is on this basis that managerial styles are classified in terms of the extent to which managers allow their subordinates the opportunity to participate in decision-making. Thus, styles can range from the highly autocratic ('You solve the problem or make the decision yourself, using information available to you at the time') to the highly participative ('You share the problem with your subordinates as a group. Together you generate and evaluate alternatives and attempt to reach agreement (consensus) on a solution. Your role is much like that of a chairman. You do not try to influence the group to adopt your solution, and you are willing to accept and implement any solution which has the support of the entire group').

Contextual modelling and analysis.   Having formulated the objectives he wishes to achieve by tackling a particular problem, and having classified the alternatives that are the focus of the exercise, the manager must now consider the context in which the eventual choice is to apply.

To some extent the 'relevant' context is self-defining, given the nature of the objectives sought and the focus of the problem-solving exercise. Thus, at one level, the context of a payment system, or for that matter, a managerial style, is that group of workers to whom it is applied, or who act it out. This comprises a quickly identifiable tangible context. At another level, though, the relevant context may be characterized as that range of

Group Problems	Individual Problems
A1. You solve the problem or make the decision yourself, using information available to you at the time	A1. You solve the problem or make the decision by yourself, using information available to you at the time
A11. You obtain the necessary information from your subordinates, then decide the solution to the problem yourself. You may or may not tell your subordinates what the problem is in getting the information from them. The role played by your subordinates in making the decision is clearly one of providing the necessary information to you, rather than generating or evaluating alternative solutions	A11. You obtain the necessary information from your subordinate, then decide on the solution to the problem yourself. You may or may not tell the subordinate what the problem is in getting the information from him. His role in making the decision is clearly one of providing the necessary information to you, rather than generating or evaluating alternative solutions
C1. You share the problem with the relevant subordinates individually, getting their ideas and suggestions without bringing them together as a group. Then *you* make the decision, which may or may not reflect your subordinates' influence	C1. You share the problem with your subordinate, getting his ideas and suggestions. Then you make a decision, which may or may not reflect his influence
C11. You share the problem with your subordinates as a group, obtaining their collective ideas and suggestions. Then you make the decision, which may or may not reflect your subordinates' influence	G1. You share the problem with your subordinate, and together you analyse the problem and arrive at a mutually agreeable solution
G11. You share the problem with your subordinates as a group. Together you generate and evaluate alternatives and attempt to reach agreement (consensus) on a solution. Your role is much like that of chairman. You do not try to influence the group to adopt 'your' solution, and you are willing to accept and implement any solution which has the support of the entire group	D1. You delegate the problem to your subordinate, providing him with any relevant information that you possess, but giving him responsibility for solving the problem by himself. You may or may not request him to tell you what solution he has reached

Figure 5.4. Decision methods for group and individual problems (After Vroom and Yetton (1973), Table 2.1)

factors, and their inter-relationships, which it is hypothesized impinge directly upon the operation of the payment system or the use of a particular managerial style. These may be as broad as the organization itself (e.g., 'organizational context'), or characterize a particular set of structures and processes within the organization (e.g., the manufacturing process), or comprise the attributes of different types of interpersonal situation (e.g., committee meetings, project management groups). The *type* of factors seen as relevant to specifying context will depend on the meta theory used initially to identify and define a particular order of problems (e.g., 'structural' problems, or 'interpersonal' problems), while the precise nature of the problem (e.g., a payment system that is facilitating productivity drift) will select specific aspects of a generally delineated context for emphasis.

The procedure developed by Lupton and Gowler to specify the context of a wage payment system well illustrates this approach. As they themselves point out, the meta theory that informs their perspective on organizational analysis and problem-identification is that of open systems analysis used in the development of 'mutual causation' or feedback models (1969, appendix B; Shanin, 1972, page 12). With this orientation, their first step was to construct a general socio-technical systems model of the factors affecting manpower planning and utilization in an organization's performance of its focal task (see Fig. 5.5). This model, described in another paper (Gowler 1969), shows the inter-relationships between seven variables, namely (a) market/client demands (b) product/service changes (c) production/servicing arrangements (d) job requirements (e) the demand for labour (f) job expectations (g) the supply of labour. While the dotted arrows in Fig. 5.5 show the *logic* of the manufacturing/servicing situation, the solid arrows represent its *dynamic* (for explication, see Gowler, 1969, pages 75–76). Context is represented here in sufficiently broad terms to allow for its general application to a wide range of person-

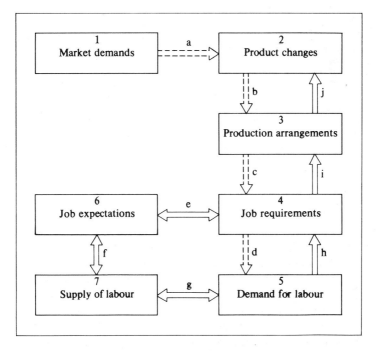

Figure 5.5. A model of organizational context (After Gowler (1969), Fig. 1)

nel management problems, including, for example, manpower planning, recruitment, and training.[7] It is from this basic model that Lupton and Gowler then derive a representation of the specific context of a wage payment system, namely the 21 dimensions, and their hypothesized relationships (see 1969, appendix B) that comprise the situational aspects or 'profile' of whatever unit is selected for which a payment system is to be designed (see Fig. 5.6). To ascertain the shape of a unit's 'profile', each scaled dimension is scored for the unit under examination, the emerging configuration representing the context relevant to the unit's payment system.

Mumford's approach to modelling context is similar. Influenced by the meta theory of Parsonian structural-functionalism, she also characterizes organizational context in terms of a socio-technical systems model, the key variables comprising product market (including market demand, stability of demand, competitor behaviour), technology, administrative functions, and structure, and organizational culture (norms and attitudes about appropriate behaviour). The inter-relationships she hypothesizes between them, in fact, comprise a general model of organization similar to that which informs Lupton and Gowler's analysis (see Fig. 5.5). In terms of a job design exercise to meet the objectives of employee job satisfaction and organizational efficiency, this general model of context is related to the job requirements and job expectations (identified in the objective setting exercise) of specific work groups for whom job redesign is to be undertaken.

Vroom and Yetton's approach to characterizing the contexts relevant to the exercise of each of their five decision-making styles, although similar in theory, contains some important differences. Again, a meta theory, the social psychology of decision-making, directs their identification and choice of relevant contextual variables. Yet, this theory inclines them towards a narrow definition of context. The unit for the analysis of context is derived directly from a consideration of the three classes of outcomes that influence the ultimate effectiveness of decisions, namely the quality or rationality of the decision, the acceptance of the decision by subordinates and their commitment to execute it effectively, and the amount of time required to make the decision. Thus, context is defined in terms of two types of problem attributes: those which specify the importance for a particular problem of quality and acceptance and those which, on the basis of available evidence, have a high probability of moderating the effects of participation on each of these outcomes. From this analysis of context in terms of problem attributes, eight diagnostic questions are derived (see

[7] Examples of how this model has been developed and used as a basis for analysing problems of manpower development and utilization may be found in Gowler and Legge, 1973a; Legge 1974.

1 (g) Type of effort	TIME			ENERGY			COMPETENCE			
2 (g) Unit of accountability	INDIVIDUAL			GROUP			PLANT			
	1	2	3	4	5	6	7	8	9	
1 Length of job cycle	to 5	6–10	11–15	16–30	31–45	46–60	61–90	91–120	121+	Mins.
2 Number of job modifications	0	1	2	3	4	5	6	7	8+	Av. no. per month
3 Degree of automation	SPT	PAT	SMT	CMT	STM	CTM	SPO	CPO	CCP	
4 Number of product changes	0	1	2	3	4	5	6	7	8+	Av. no. per month
5 Number of job stoppages	0	1	2	3	4	5	6	7	8+	Av. no. per day
6 Duration of job stoppages	0	1–5	6–10	11–20	21–30	31–40	41–50	51–60	61+	Av. no. mins. per day
7 % job elements specified by management	71+	61–70	51–60	41–50	31–40	21–30	11–20	1–10	0	%
8 % material scrapped	0	1–2	3–4	5–6	7–8	9–10	11–12	13–14	15+	%
9 Products/components rejected	0	1–2	3–4	5–6	7–8	9–10	11–12	13–14	15+	%
10 Time required to fill vacancy	1	2–4	5–7	8–10	11–13	14–16	17–19	20–22	23+	Days
11 Labour stability	81+	71–80	61–70	51–60	41–50	31–40	21–30	11–20	0–10	%
12 Labour turnover	0	6	12	18	24	30	36	42	48	Men %
	0	12	24	36	48	60	72	84	96	Women %
13 Disputes about pay	0–4	5–8	9–12	13–16	17–20	21–24	25–28	29–32	33+	Av. no. per month
14 Man hours lost in pay disputes	0–4	5–8	9–12	13–16	17–20	21–24	25–28	29–32	33+	% per month
15 % earnings decided outside plant/company	0–10	11–20	21–30	31–40	41–50	51–60	61–70	71–80	81+	%
16 Number of trade unions	0	1–3	4–6	7–9	10–12	13–15	16–18	19–21	22+	All plant
17 Occupational structure	0–3	4–6	7–9	10–12	13–15	16–18	19–21	22–24	25+	All plant
18 Absence	0	2–3	4–5	6–7	8–9	10–11	12–13	14–15	16+	% normal hours
19 Average age of working force		15–29			30–44			45+		Years
20 % labour cost in unit cost	23+	21–23	18–20	15–17	12–14	10–12	7–9	4–6	1–3	%
21 % males in working force	0	to 10	11–20	21–30	31–40	41–50	51–60	61–70	71+	All plant

Figure 5.6. Profile blank (After Lupton and Gowler (1969), Fig. 4)

109

A. If decision were accepted, would it make a difference which course of action were adopted?

B. Do I have sufficient information to make a high quality decision?

C. Do subordinates have sufficient additional information to result in a high quality decision?

D. Do I know exactly what information is needed, who possesses it, and how to collect it?

E. Is acceptance of decision by subordinates critical to effective implementation?

F. If I were to make the decision by myself, is it certain that it would be accepted by my subordinates?

G. Can subordinates be trusted to base solutions on organizational considerations?

H. Is conflict among subordinates likely in preferred solutions?

Figure 5.7. Problem attributes as the context of managerial decision-making (After Vroom and Yetton (1973), Table 2.3)

Fig. 5.7) by which a manager may define the nature of the problem he has to cope with—in other words the immediate context to which he has to apply a particular decision-making style. What Vroom and Yetton do not undertake, although they recognize the need for it, is to model the types of organizational circumstances that give rise to different problem types, resulting ultimately in different distributions of problem types which, in aggregate, may require different modal styles or levels of participation (1973, page 19). Nor do they explicitly model the dynamic inter-relationships between their eight problem attributes, although this is compensated for by their procedure for matching decision-making style to type of context/problem, as will be discussed below.

'Matching' alternatives choices to context. Having classified a range of alternative choices (whether payment systems, or ways in which jobs can be structured, or decision-making styles) and characterized their relevant contexts, the next step is to match the one with the other in a way that will facilitate the achievement of the initially specified objectives. Both Lupton and Gowler and Vroom and Yetton provide particularly good illustrations of how this can be done.

Lupton and Gowler's technique is as follows. Having characterized the context in which a payment system is to operate through a configuration of scores on the situational profile (Fig. 5.6), they then match it to a particular wage payment system through relating the scores on the dimensions to the appropriate types of effort, reward and effort-reward relationships discussed above (see Fig. 5.8). This 'matching' procedure then relates the types of payment systems characterized by certain types of effort-reward relationships to the different types of situation, represented by the profile scores obtained for a situation. For example, following Fig. 5.8, a low score on the length of job cycle dimension (dimension 1) would indicate that the effort-reward relationship appropriate to a short job cycle is reciprocal

	Type of effort	TIME			ENERGY			COMPETENCE			
1 (g)	Type of effort	INDIVIDUAL			GROUP			PLANT			
2 (g)	Unit of Accountability	1	2	3	4	5	6	7	8	9	
		3RI	2RI	1RI	3RD	2RD	1RD	1NR	2NR	3NR	
1	Length of job cycle	to5	6–10	11–15	16–30	31–45	46–60	61–90	91–120	121+	Mins.
		3RI	2RI	1RI	3RD	2RD	1RD	1NR	2NR	3NR	
2	Number of job modifications	0	1	2	3	4	5	6	7	8+	Av. no. per month
		3RI	2RI	1RI	3RD	2RD	1RD	1NR	2NR	3NR	
3	Degree of Automation	SPT	PAT	SMT	CMT	STM	CTM	SPO	CPO	CCP	
		3RI	2RI	1RI	3RD	2RD	1RD	1NR	2NR	3NR	
4	Number of product changes	0	1	2	3	4	5	6	7	8+	Av. no. per month
		3RI	2RI	1RI	3RD	2RD	1RD	1NR	2NR	3NR	
5	Number of job stoppages	0	1	2	3	4	5	6	7	8+	Av. no. per day
		3RI	2RI	1RI	3RD	2RD	1RD	1NR	2NR	3NR	
6	Duration of job stoppages	0	1–5	6–10	11–20	21–30	31–40	41–50	51–60	61+	Av. no mins. per day
		3RI	2RI	1RI	3RD	2RD	1RD	1NR	2NR	3NR	
7	% job elements specified by management	71+	61–70	51–60	41–50	31–40	21–30	11–20	1–10	0	%
		3RI	2RI	1RI	3RD	2RD	1RD	1NR	2NR	3NR	
8	% material scrapped	0	1–2	3–4	5–6	7–8	9–10	11–12	13–14	15+	%
		3RI	2RI	1RI	3RD	2RD	1RD	1NR	2NR	3NR	
9	% product/components rejected	0	1–2	3–4	5–6	7–8	9–10	11–12	12–14	15+	%
		3RI	2RI	IRI	3RD	2RD	IRD	1NR	2NR	3NR	
10	Time required to fill vacancy	1	2–4	5–7	8–10	11–13	14–16	17–19	20–22	23+	Days
		3RI	2RI	1RI	3RD	2RD	1RD	1NR	2NR	3NR	
11	Labout stability	81+	71–80	61–70	51–60	41–50	31–40	21–30	11–20	to 10	%
		3RI	2RI	1RI	3RD	2RD	1RD	1NR	2NR	3NR	
12	Labour turnover	0	6	12	18	24	30	36	42	48	Men %
		0	12	24	36	48	60	72	84	96	Women %
		3RI	2RI	1RI	3RD	2RD	1RD	1NR	2NR	3NR	
13	Disputes about pay	0–4	5–8	9–12	13–16	17–20	21–24	25–28	29–32	33+	Av. no. per month
		3RI	2RI	1RI	3RD	2RD	1RD	1NR	2NR	3NR	
14	Man hours lost in pay disputes	0–4	5–8	9–12	13–16	17–20	21–24	25–28	29–32	33+	% per month
		3RI	2RI	1RI	3RD	2RD	1RD	1NR	2NR	3NR	
15	% earnings decided outside plant/company	0–10	11–20	21–30	31–40	41–50	51–60	61–70	71–80	81+	%
		3RI	2RI	1RI	3RD	2RD	1RD	1NR	2NR	3NR	
16	Number of trade unions	0	1–3	4–6	7–9	10–12	13–15	16–18	19–21	22+	All plant
		3RI	2RI	1RI	3RD	2RD	1RD	1NR	2NR	3NR	
17	Occupational structure	0–3	4–6	7–9	10–12	13–15	16–18	19–21	22–24	24+	All plant
		3RI	2RI	1RI	3RD	2RD	1RD	1NR	2NR	3NR	
18	Absence	0	2–3	4–5	6–7	8–9	10–11	12–13	14–15	16+	% normal hours
			3RI			3RD			3NR			
19	Average age of working force		15–29			30–44			45+			Years
		3RD	2RI	1RI	3RD	2RD	1RD	1NR	2NR	3NR	
20	% labour cost in unit cost	23+	21–23	18–20	15–17	12–14	10–12	7–9	4–6	1–3	%
		3RI	2RI	1RI	3RD	2RD	1RD	1NR	2NR	3NR	
21	% males in working force	0	to 10	11–20	21–30	31–40	41–50	51–60	61–70	71+	% All plant

Figure 5.8. Payment systems master block (After Lupton and Gowler (1969), Fig. 5)

immediate (RI), while a high score on this dimension suggests that a non-reciprocal (NR) reward is appropriate to a long job cycle. Similarly, where the number of job stoppages is high, non-reciprocal (NR) rewards would seem far more appropriate than reciprocal immediate (RI) rewards. In other words, one would have to question the wisdom of applying an incentive method of payment in these circumstances.

Few units are likely to offer a completely homogeneous context (i.e., where the different dimensions are scored as appropriate to just one type of effort-reward relationship). Typically, a short job cycle, suggesting the appropriateness of a reciprocal immediate (RI) relationship, may be offset by a high score on dimension 10 'time required to fill a vacancy', suggesting that a non-reciprocal (NR) relationship might be more appropriate, while the score on, say, 'level of absence', may suggest a reciprocal deferred (RD) effort-reward relationship. In these circumstances, Lupton and Gowler suggest that the manager has three lines of approach.

First, if the majority of the dimensions and particularly the technological dimensions suggest one type of effort-reward relationship, he may consider that the advantages of simplicity in administration outweigh any disadvantages of ignoring the other types of effort-reward relationship indicated, and that a 'pure' method of payment is preferable to a hybrid system. In these circumstances, he must assess in what ways the 'misfit' dimensions might undermine the smooth operation of the selected payment system and, if these are likely to prove significant, how to cope with the dysfunctional 'side-effects'.

Second, if the scores on most dimensions point to one form of effort-reward relationship, or if, in spite of 'misfit' dimensions, management wishes to retain an existing payment system, although along several dimensions it would appear inappropriate, Lupton and Gowler suggest that the following approach may be used. Instead of trying to modify the payment system to fit the dimensions better, it may be appropriate to alter the score on some dimensions to suit the existing payment system. Thus, for example, if the scores on the technological dimensions would appear to indicate the retention of an energy reciprocal immediate scheme (i.e., an incentive bonus scheme), but the scheme is being undermined by high labour turnover and absence, the best policy may be for management to analyse the causes of such behaviours, and act to change them. If management does decide on this second line of approach, i.e., that adjusting the dimensions rather than the method of payment is appropriate, care must be taken to estimate the influence that one dimension is exercising upon another as well as that of the existing payment system on the profile as a whole. For example, if over a period of time the number of product changes has increased drastically, so much so that a situational score previously appropriate to a reciprocal immediate (RI) effort-reward relationship, has been transformed into a score more appropriate to a non-reciprocal (NR) effort-reward relationship, the operation of, say, an

ERI based payment system may well be undermined, resulting in labour turnover and absence.[8]

The third approach to matching payment system and situation appropriately, when the scores on the dimensions suggest a range of appropriate effort-reward relationships, is to design a 'hybrid' payment system. In doing so, Lupton and Gowler point out, it is necessary for management to consider these 'matches' in the light of the objectives it hopes to achieve through each element, and the objectives it hopes to achieve from the 'hybrid' payment system as a whole. For, it may well be that the behaviours evoked by some elements in the pay packet may militate against the achievement of objectives to be elicited through other elements. Thus, the working of overtime to increase output, elicited by rates higher than time rates (TRI), may undermine the speed of performance (and hence output) achieved through the incentive element (ERI) of the 'hybrid' payment system, as the worker 'paces' himself throughout the day. Management, therefore, will have to consider the mutual compatibility of the elements in a hybrid system, and what might be the appropriate size of each element, in the light of its objectives. (One method of doing this can be found in Bowey and Lupton, 1970.)

The key to Lupton and Gowler's approach here is the logic that allows context to be characterized by scores that can be translated directly into various types of effort-reward relationship. In other words, the implicit rules that relate context (the independent variable) to payment system (the dependent variable) are embedded in the procedure itself. Vroom and Yetton's approach differs only in that they provide a set of seven explicit rules, distinct from, but related to, their characterization of context and managerial styles of decision-making, in order to match the one with the other through a process of elimination (see 1973, pages 32–37). These rules are designed to protect both the quality and acceptance of a decision. An example of the former is the 'information rule', which states that if the quality of the decision is important and if the manager does not possess enough information or expertise to solve the problem himself, the highly

---

[8] It should be noted that while the *normative* contingent assumption behind the Lupton–Gowler method of selecting a payment system is that it is a *dependent* variable (i.e., its design and appropriateness is dependent—and should be dependent—upon the characteristics of the situation in which it is to operate), the variables that comprise the dimensions of the situational profile (and the scores obtained on them) are obviously influenced by the existing payment system, acting *independently* upon them. For example, an existing inappropriate payment system may well influence markedly the scores on such dimensions as, for example, 12, 13, 14, 18, 19, 20, and influence the scores on other dimensions indirectly. If the scores on the technological dimensions (dimensions 1 to 9 and especially 1, 3, 7) indicate that the existing payment system is inappropriate to these dimensions, it may well be that the scores on some of the other dimensions partly reflect this inappropriateness. To ascertain the independent effect of a payment system upon organizational context as represented by these variables, as well as *vice versa*, demands the use of contingency theory, in its *positive/descriptive* sense—as illustrated in Fig. 5.5.

authoritarian decision style (i.e., 'you solve the problem or make the decision yourself, using the information available to you at the time') can be eliminated as inappropriate. Alternatively, an example of the acceptance protecting type of decision rule, is the basic 'acceptance rule'. Namely, that if the acceptance of the decision by subordinates is critical to effective implementation, and if it is not certain that an autocratic decision made by a manager would receive that acceptance, all decision making styles that do not involve consultation and/or group decision-making are eliminated.

To match context (or nature of the problem) with decision-making style, these rules should be used in conjunction with diagnozing the nature of the problem. In other words, the problem should be characterized according to its quality and acceptance attributes, which in turn should be examined in the light of the decision rules to ascertain which decision styles are thereby eliminated, and which consequently remain acceptable. To facilitate this diagnostic process, Vroom and Yetton suggest that it may be represented as a decision tree. This enables the problem/context to be characterized not just by a list, but by a configuration of attributes. To take two examples. If, in characterizing a problem, the answer to question A 'If decision were accepted, would it make a difference which course of action were adopted' is 'no', the subsidiary questions about the quality requirements (see Fig. 5.7) of the situation become irrelevant, and it remains to ask the basic acceptance question 'Is acceptance of decision by subordinates critical to effective implementation?' If the answer to this is also 'no', the context is characterized as insensitive to both quality and acceptance requirements, in which case, none of the decision rules apply and all the decision-making styles are theoretically appropriate. In such circumstances, the decision style then selected is that which requires the least investment in manhours, i.e., the highly authoritarian style, unless other criteria (such as development needs of subordinates) are employed. Alternatively, if the answer to question A ('If decision were accepted, would it make a difference which course of action were adopted?') was 'yes', the manager would have to consider question B, 'Do I have sufficient information to make a high quality decision?'. If the answer was in fact 'yes', he could then proceed to the acceptance questions, but if the answer was 'no', questions C and D (about his subordinates' information and about the degree of structure in the problem) would have to be considered. If the answer to question C was 'yes', but to 'D' was 'no', and if the answer to the basic acceptance question E was also 'no', then by relating this information to the decision rules, and by using them to ascertain which styles were thereby eliminated, the manager is left with the consultative and group decision-making styles as feasible alternatives. Of these two, the consultative style may be preferred if the minimum manhours criterion is applied. Readers requiring a detailed exposition of this process are referred to the authors' own account (1973, Chapter 3).

Evaluation processes.   Finally, a contingent approach involves evaluation processes at the two levels. First, what is the overall success of the exercise in terms of outcome? Have the new payment system or the redesigned jobs achieved the objectives set for them and at what cost? Which objectives have been achieved and which have been lost? While *post facto* monitoring is clearly important here, in particular to assess the effect of subsequent environmental or organizational changes on context and, hence, on the redesigned system, evaluation procedures also need to be an integral part of the design exercise while it is still continuing. In particular, some evaluation needs to take place not only in terms of which alternative will best achieve a given objective, but on what basis trade-offs should take place between objectives, and whether the theoretically appropriate alternative is practically easy to implement. Thus, Mumford proposes that, prior to selection, each job redesign proposed is initially vetted for both 'human' and 'efficiency' advantages or disadvantages, that if there is conflict here, criteria must be established to determine which objectives should be given priority and on what basis compromise should be reached (1976, pages 35–36). Similarly, Lupton and Gowler suggest, through their use of a Potentiality–Difficulty grid (1969, Fig. 6), that the priority among the different objectives that could be sought by use of a payment system, and the issues involved in implementing a new system aimed at selected objectives, should be assessed in terms to their potential pay off for cost saving in relation to their potential difficulty in implementing.

Apart from this, a contingent approach also requires an evaluation of the actual procedures designed to select the outcome, be it payment system, redesigned job or managerial style, so that they may be made increasingly effective. The method used by Vroom and Yetton for validating and refining their procedure provides some useful insights on how this may be done (1973, Chapter 9), while Lupton and Gowler's approach has been tested and to some extent refined by Gillispie (1973b).

Conclusions

A contingent approach to problem-solving brings with it the combined advantages of flexibility (which allows for its application to most areas of personnel, indeed, management activity) with a sensitivity to the political dimensions of organizational life. On the one hand, its emphasis on the design and evaluation of changes in the light of preferred objectives is consistent with the manager's need to match his activities (and their outcomes) with recognized success criteria, in order to develop credibility and gain power and influence within the organization. On the other hand, the approach is in tune with recent trends towards the democratization of the workplace. For, as both Lupton and Gowler and Mumford point out, participation on the part of multi-functional management groups, with representatives of all those employees who are to be affected by the proposed changes, is the logical answer to the need to gain the range and depth of information and perspectives that are essential for the development of realistic models of organizational context, appropriate forms of organizational design, and their implementation.

Only three examples of this approach have been discussed here, but other examples of the practical application, rather than pious invocation, of this approach can be found. For example, in relation to flexible working hours there is the work of Legge (1974) and Lee and McEwan Young (1977), or in relation to the use of overtime, there is the work of Brown (1969) or in relation to participation that of Donaldson and Gowler (1975) and that of Morse and Lorsch (1970), or even in relation to what might appear trivial issues, like suggestion schemes, that of Gorfin (1969). The flexibility of this approach is particularly appropriate to the personnel manager as problem-solver.

6. A contingent approach to personnel management: II

In the previous chapter, it was argued that the personnel specialist (or for that matter, any manager) in the role of 'organizational diagnostician' might usefully adopt a contingent approach in tackling key areas of organizational design relating to personnel management. Can this approach similarly be applied to that area of organizational design that involves him directly, namely the design of the personnel function?

Obviously, to use contingency theory as an approach to the design and management of key substantive areas of personnel management *is* virtually synonymous with using it to design the personnel function, if the latter is taken in its broadest activity, based sense (i.e., 'the optimum utilization of human resources in the pursuit of organizational goals'). But, quite apart from the detailed illustrations of this approach, is it now possible to suggest some more general guidelines as to how a manager's approach to personnel activities might take account of organizational context? Further, if the 'personnel function' is taken to mean the institutionalized presence of that activity (i.e., the personnel department), the design activity involved must focus additionally on the development of roles and relationships and the delineation of areas of responsibility and modes of operation appropriate to a specialist department operating in a particular context (cf., Foulkes and Morgan, 1977). Put this way, it is clear that both exercises involve several unresolved problems, not least of which is the perennial difficulty of modelling organizational context in a way appropriate to the issues in hand. It is to this question that we now return.

Organizational context

For the purposes in hand, organizational context may be considered at two levels. First, what are the key variables that are likely to influence, if not determine, both organizational culture (the shared beliefs and values about such things as the way 'work should be organized, the way authority exercised, people rewarded, controlled, etc.'), and the resulting regular behaviour patterns that characterize an organization? What are the inter-relationships between these variables? Second, how may the resulting 'organizational cultures' and patterns of behaviour themselves be characterized? (cf., Lussato, 1976). Finally, what is the relationship between these two representations of organizational context?

The approach adopted here rests on the work of the Aston School (Pugh *et al.*, 1968); Payne and Pugh 1976; Harrison 1972; Lawrence and Lorsch (1967a) and that of Handy (1976), quite apart from the ever prevalent influence of the work of Gowler and Lupton and others at the Manchester Business School (Lupton and Gowler, 1969; Gowler, 1969; Lupton, 1970). (For an alternative, if similar, approach to modelling organizational context, see Shortell, 1977.)

What factors, then, influence the development of a particular organizational culture and resulting behaviour patterns? Following the Aston School and Handy, it is suggested that six factors are of crucial importance, namely:

History and ownership
Size
Technology
Goals and objectives
The environment
Potential employees

Before considering how exactly these factors may influence organizational culture and behaviour, two points must be borne in mind. First, that the concepts itemized above are really multi-dimensional, umbrella-like terms for clusters of variables, and that in any model-building hypothesis-generating exercise it may be necessary to differentiate which aspect of the concept is thought to affect a particular aspect of behaviour. Thus, for example, in using a concept like 'environment', it is necessary to consider what variables it comprises, and a long list may be drawn up (e.g., product market, including customers' requirements and the strategies of competitors; labour market, including the number and availability of potential employees, the strategies of competitors to attract this labour; the scientific knowledge environment; the political, legislative and societal environment, and so on).[1] Second, that even having carefully defined the

---

[1] The last two aspects of the environment could in turn be considered as characteristics of product and labour markets respectively.

components of these concepts, they cannot then be used just as a checklist of factors each separately influencing organizational culture and behaviour patterns. Such an approach would tend to overlook the possibility that each factor may pull in a different direction and that, as a consequence, it might be the nature of their inter-relationships just as much as their individual characteristics that determines their overall effect on dependent behaviour (Gowler and Legge, 1973a). Hence, not only is a model-building exercise called for, but one in which the recognition exists that an organization may be represented by several different models, depending on which aspects of these global concepts are operationalized, and to which parts of the organization (or organizational problems) it is to be applied.

By way of example, the Lupton–Gowler model used earlier provides basically an illustration of this approach, and an amended version to accommodate aspects of all six factors is provided in Fig. 6.1. It will be noted that some of the Lupton–Gowler variables are, in fact, components of the multi-dimensional concepts, as when 'environment' is operationalized in terms of product and labour market. Further illustrations of the

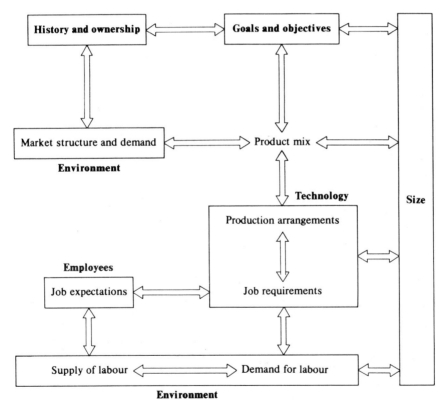

Figure 6.1. The Lupton–Gowler model amended to incorporate six key factors (Handy (1976))

119

multi-dimensional nature of the six factors may be found in Appendix I, and another illustration of how they may be used in a model-building exercise is provided later in the argument.

Before we can turn to the relationship between organizational context, as expressed in models of these six factors, and organizational context, as expressed in models of organizational culture and patterns of activity, it is necessary to characterize the latter. Here, the work of Handy (1976) and Harrison (1972) may prove useful. Basically, Handy argues that the patterns of activity in organizations, resulting from the interaction of the six factors cited above, may be characterized under four headings:

> *Steady-state*—those activities which can be programmed in some way and are routine as opposed to non-routine.
> *Innovative/developmental*—those activities which are directed at changing the things that the organization does or the way it does them.
> *Breakdown/crises*—those activities designed to cope with the unprogrammed and unexpected.
> *Policy/direction*—those activities concerned with the setting of priorities, the establishment of standards, the direction and allocation of resources, the initiation of action.[2]

Further Handy suggests that each of these sets of activities has a culture appropriate to it, namely:

> Steady-state activities—a *role* culture.
> Innovative/developmental activities—a *task* culture.
> Breakdown/crises activities—a *power* culture.
> Policy/direction activities—a *power* culture.

These cultures, or shared beliefs about the way the organization (or a department within it) should be managed and operate, and which Handy derives from the work of Harrison (1972), may be characterized as follows:

The *power* ideology, frequently found in small entrepreneurial organizations, 'depends on a central power source, with rays of power and influence spreading out from that central figure' (Handy, 1976, page 178). In an organization typified by this culture, there are few written rules and procedures, control being exercised by the centre 'largely through the selection of key individuals, by occasional forays from the centre or summonses to the centre' (page 178). Such organizations depend heavily on the quality of the individuals at the centre and hence on their ability to cope well with the succession issue. The emphasis on the individual and the lack of formalized procedures is reflected in the lack of faith in committees and the emphasis on results, irrespective of means. Decision-making tends to be in the hands of those individuals whose power base is resource, rather than expert power, and/or charismatic power, at least at the centre. All this contributes to a competitive, risk-taking working environment. The

---

[2] Morris (1972) has suggested a similar classification of activities.

strength of such an organization is its speed of reaction to environmental change, although the quality of decisions made in this area will very much depend on the culture of the people at the centre. Its weakness is that it has difficulty in coping with a growth in size, as this may place too much pressure on the non-formalized control systems, and on the maintenance of consensus upon which this type of organizational culture relies. The old Slater Walker empire would be a good example of such an organizational culture.

The *role* ideology is that which is typified by functional specialization and control and co-ordination through formal rules and procedures, resting on the hierarchical principle. In other words, the ideology is of a bureaucratic nature. In organizations typified by this ideology, the role to be filled is the focus of attention rather than the individual who is to fill it. 'Individuals are selected for a satisfactory (not superlative) performance of a role, and the role is usually so described that a range of individuals could fill it . . . the efficiency of this culture depends on the rationality of the allocation of work and responsibility rather than on individual personalities' (Handy, 1976, page 180). Thus, position power tends to be the main power source in such a culture, backed up to some extent by expert power but 'only in its proper place'. Charismatic power is considered inappropriate. This ideology, generally speaking, offers security and predictability to its employees, and 'the chance to acquire specialist expertise without risk' (page 181). It does not favour a pursuit of results at the expense of unorthodox methods.

The role ideology tends to prosper in a stable environment where the organization can control market demands through its monopolistic or oligopolistic position (such as the oil and chemical industries, the Civil Service, the public utilities), or its ability to capitalize on long product life cycles (such as life insurance companies, Electricity Boards). Similarly, 'role organization will be found where economies of scale are more important than flexibility or where technical expertise and depth of specialization are more important than product innovation or product cost' (Handy, 1976, page 181), and where emphasis is placed on product (or service) reliability rather than innovation. Conversely, the slowness of organizations typified by this ideology, in both perceiving and reacting to environmental change, can periodically lead to their collapse and takeover by organizations more responsive to environmental demands (e.g., the British motor industry in the 1960s).

The *task* ideology is job or project orientated, and organizations with this culture tend to develop a 'matrix organization' type structure. As the emphasis is on task achievement, expert power tends to be more important than position or charismatic power (at least when markets are buoyant) and 'to this end the culture seeks to bring together the appropriate resources, the right people at the right level of the organization and to let them get on with it' (Handy 1976, page 182). As a result, a team culture tends to predominate, where individuals subordinate their own objectives and attachment to their formal status to the achievement of the team's objective, and in return have the satisfaction of a high degree of control over their work and recognition on the basis of task achievement. The exercise of day-to-day control over the work team's methods of working and procedures tends to be slack, as they are considered the experts, close to the ground, who 'know best', but, in the long term, 'control is retained by top management by an allocation of projects, people and resources' (page 182) to those project leaders with a proven record of success.

The task ideology tends to flourish where 'the market is competitive, where the product life is short, and where speed of reaction and sensitivity to environmental change is important'. Although this culture may pervade the whole of an organization (e.g., an advertising agency, general management consultancy agency), it may also predominate in those departments of organizations with a role culture, which have a particular responsibility for innovation or development (e.g., the R and D Department, the computing services department, product groups of marketing departments). However, the adaptability of organizations typified by this ideology, where the norm is for 'groups, project teams or task forces (to be) formed for a specific purpose, and (later) . . . reformed, abandoned or continued' (Handy 1976, page 182), carries with it the cost that economies of scale may be lost, as well as that depth of expertise that is the product of specialization.

This ideology tends to weaken if confronted by adverse market conditions and financial constraints. For, 'when resources are not available to all who can justify their needs for them, when money and people have to be rationed, top management begins to feel the need to control methods as well as results' (Handy, 1976, page 183). In addition, project leaders are likely to start competing for available resources and in this situation, the use of expert power may become supplemented (if not supplanted) by that of position and resource power. Similarly, if, as it is likely, a drop in morale occurs among the project teams, such power may have to be employed to get work out that previously was a natural product of the supportive environment. Thus, as Handy points out, 'the task culture tends to change to a role or power culture when resources are limited or the total organization is unsuccessful' (page 183).

Even to describe these three different cultures, there is a need to suggest some of the likely relationships between them and organizational context in terms of the variables in the six-factor model.[3] Handy, in fact, goes further and, depending on how the concept is defined, suggests how factors such as the nature of the technology, or that of potential employees, either give rise to, or are appropriate to, a particular culture. For example:

[3] For a detailed analysis of the effects of such structural variables on organizational culture and ideology (and *vice versa*), see Gowler and Legge's (1973b) study of a voluntary organization, and Abrams and McCulloch's (1976) study of communes.

Studies of technology . . . do not . . . obviously point towards one or other of the cultures, but:

1. Routine, programmable operations are more suitable to a role culture than any of the others.
2. High cost, expensive technologies, where the cost of breakdown is high, tend to encourage close monitoring and supervision and require depth of expertise. Both are more appropriate in a role culture.
3. Technologies where there are clear economies of scale by mass production of heavy capital investment tend to encourage large size and thence role cultures.
4. Non-continuous discrete operations, the one-off job, unit production, these technologies are suited to power or task cultures.
5. Rapidly changing technologies require a task or power culture to be dealt with effectively.
6. Tasks with a high degree of interdependence call for systematized co-ordination and a role culture. In markets where co-ordination and uniformity are

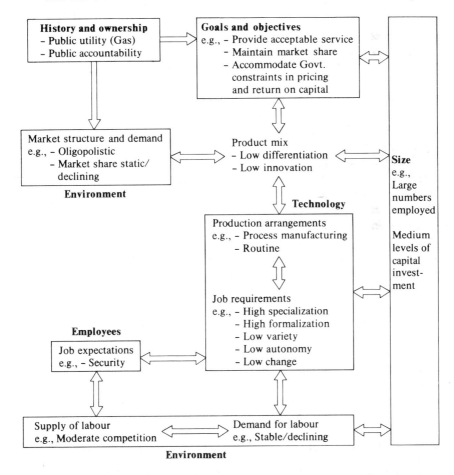

Figure 6.2. An example of an organizational context in which steady state activities and a role culture tend to prevail (Gas industry, late 1950s, early 1960s)

more important than adaptability, a role culture will therefore be appropriate (Handy, 1976, pages 189–190).

or

1. Individuals with a low tolerance for ambiguity will prefer the tighter role prescriptions of the role culture (cf., Gowler and Legge, 1972).
2. High needs for security will be better met in the role culture.
3. A need to establish one's identity at work will be appropriate in a power or task culture. In a role culture it will be seen as a 'person' orientation and thought disruptive.
4. The impact of individual skills and talents will be more marked in power and task cultures than in role. Hence, greater care needs to be paid to the selection and appraisal of individuals in these cultures.
5. Low calibre people resources—in the sense of intelligence or interpersonal skills—would push an organization towards a role culture where jobs can be defined down to the level of the manpower available[4] (Handy, 1976, page 195).

For reasons stated above, however, it is necessary to move on from this rather 'check-list' approach to the relationship between contextual variables and organizational culture, and to relate actual models of organizational context to particular activity patterns and the prevailing culture they are likely to give rise to. Such an exercise may be usefully done at both organizational and departmental levels. By way of illustration of this approach, Fig. 6.2 suggests how the interactions between the six factors may operate in a manner likely to encourage the growth and predominance of steady-state activities, and hence a role culture. Figure 6.3 suggests how changes in these factors and the nature of their interactions are likely to lead to some disruption of steady-state activities and the role culture generally. Such changes, it is suggested, may simultaneously lead to the development of innovatory activities and a task culture in one part of the organization (see Fig. 6.4) but result in breakdown/crises activities and a power culture in another (see Fig. 6.5), thus increasing the level of organizational differentiation.

Not only is it argued that organizations, and departments within them, *do* become differentiated, or develop different patterns of activities and different cultures according to the differing sets of environmental constraints and opportunities that they confront,[5] but that this differentiation

---

[4] It should be noted that the relationships Handy suggests need to be treated with some care, as within the same framework he tends to move from positive to normative statements. Compare, for example, 'X aspect of the technology will tend to encourage the development of Y culture' with 'X aspect of the technology needs Y culture to be dealt with effectively'. This difficulty reinforces the need for a model building approach, as it may be used to clarify the position that while the six factors interacting together may direct an organization (or department within it) towards a dominant culture, this may be contrary to that required for the achievement of organizational success criteria.

[5] Lawrence and Lorsch (1967a), for example, have suggested that different organizations, and departments within them, become (and should become) differentiated along the following dimensions, depending on the degree of uncertainty in their scientific, market and

Cont. next page

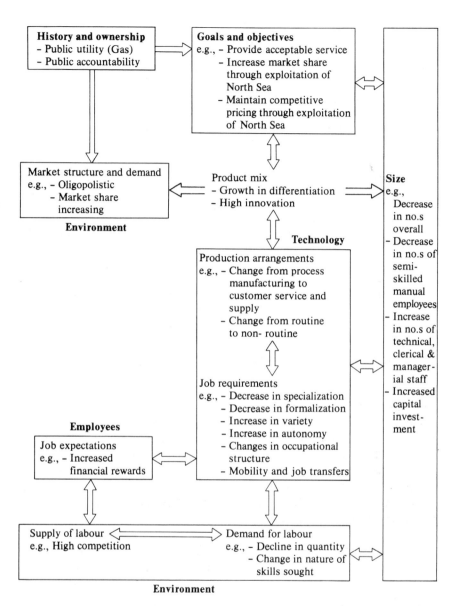

Figure 6.3. Changes in organizational context (Gas industry, late 1960s, early 1970s)

Footnote 5 (cont.)

techno-economic environments:
(a) Time horizons (long, medium or short)
(b) Orientations towards goals and objectives (e.g., customer need or product quality)
(c) Interpersonal style (e.g., task-centred, relationship-centred)
(d) Degree of formality in the structure

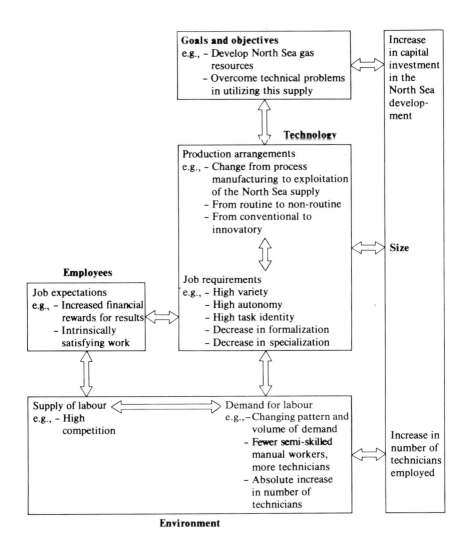

Figure 6.4. The effect on technical departments of the change in organizational context as outlined in Fig. 6.3 [**Note:** It is hypothesized that the innovatory activities would increase in the process of developing the North Sea Gas fields and that a task culture would emerge in these areas, during the period of development]

is necessary for their achievement of high performance (in terms of such factors as an increase in profits, change in sales volume and rate of product innovation in industrial organizations) (Lawrence and Lorsch, 1967a). Put another way, differentiation can be viewed from both a positive/descriptive and normative standpoint.

Bearing in mind this approach to modelling organizational context we can now turn to the design of appropriate specialist personnel departments.

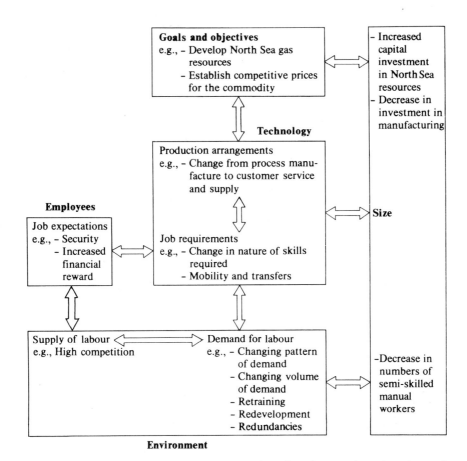

Figure 6.5. The effect on semi-skilled manual workers in manufacturing plants of the change in organizational context as outlined in Fig. 6.3 [**Note:** It is hypothesized that breakdown/crises activities would increase in the process of running down manufacturing plants and that a power culture would emerge in these areas during the period of transition]

The design of the personnel department

The modelling of organizational context presented above has implications both for the type of involvement appropriate to non-specialist managers in carrying out the personnel function, and for the design, and style of operation of a specialist personnel department itself.

On the basis of these models, it might be suggested that the activities that comprise the organization's personnel function in its broadest sense (i.e., the optimum utilization of human resources in the pursuit of organizational goals) may be differentiated according to whether they can be classified under a steady-state, innovative/developmental, breakdown/crises, policy and direction label. For example, while some aspects of management training might be classified as steady-state activities (e.g., regular programmes of graduate training and induction, the day-by-day 'on-the-job' training a boss gives to his subordinate), others might more properly be considered as innovative/developmental activities (e.g., the introduction of sensitivity training for a selected group of managers as part of an OD programme). Similarly, some aspects of industrial relations might be considered steady-state activities (e.g., line management's regular, but informal meetings with shop stewards, meetings with joint consultative councils), while others might be considered as innovative/developmental activities (e.g., the early exercises in productivity bargaining), or even breakdown/crises activities (e.g., interventions to avert or end strike action), and so on. This approach is particularly advantageous when considering what the personnel management role of the non-specialist should be, for it highlights the fact that while the manager may not be a specialist in areas of substantive personnel knowledge (e.g., recruitment and selection or manpower planning), he may properly exercise the managerial skills which he does possess, appropriate to managing a particular type of activity (i.e., steady-state, innovative, etc.), on the basis of the advice he gets as to the substantive issues involved.

Basically, in delineating where responsibility should lie for these different types of activity, management should establish what are the relevant task requirements and who is best able to meet them in terms of the resources (of knowledge, expertise, power, etc.) at their diposal in the light of conflicting priorities. Consequently, in terms of this classification, it might be that *all* managers are likely to be involved in some of the steady-state personnel activities and, in particular, line management with breakdown and crises. In these areas they will be acting in an executive role. Thus, all managers will carry out performance appraisals, and are likely to be involved, if informally, in training activities, while line managers are likely to be involved in day-to-day industrial relations activities, the implementation of pay structures, as in the authorization of overtime payments, and so on. Furthermore, it is clear from the previous chapter that managers from all functions have their own specialist perspective and input to contribute in the formulation of personnel policy and in developing innovative exercises of organizational design. Similarly, in policy formulation in their own areas, they should have the responsibility to think through its implications for specifically personnel policy and practice, possibly by inviting the participation of personnel specialists in such an exercise. The role of personnel specialists in relation to these 'personnel' activities of other management groups should be largely to establish guidelines and set parameters for their action. For example, personnel specialists should be in a position to establish with management in all functions what questions the latter should ask about the implications of their own policies and activities for those of personnel. Moreover, they should be able to audit management's use of regular personnel procedures (such as appraisal schemes).

Activity based expertise

Substantive expertise	Steady-state activities	Innovative/ developmental activities	Breakdown/ crises activities	Policy/ direction activities
Manpower planning				
Recruitment and selection				
Appraisal and evaluation				
Training				
Wage and salary administration				
Industrial relations				
Management development				
Organization development				
Organization design				
Welfare				

Figure 6.6. A framework for the design of a personnel department

In designing a specialist personnel department, whether to operate at plant, divisional or Head Office level, it is suggested that a similar approach should be applied. First, it should be considered which aspects of personnel management are most appropriately undertaken by specialists, given the resources available and the constraints and opportunities afforded by the organizational context. These activities may then be grouped according to both the substantive expertise (e.g., 'management development' or 'industrial relations') and to the relevant processual skills required, (i.e., the skills involved in managing the four different types of activity, for example the skills involved in handling strike situations, such as those possessed by the trouble shooter).[6] In other words, specialist roles may be designed on a matrix principle[7] as illustrated in Fig. 6.6. Obviously, depending on organizational requirements and the resources available, a selection may be made from the great number of specialist roles that are logically possible and, in practice, it will be necessary for each organization to decide what

[6] For an analysis of the managerial skills involved in handling maintenance, development and breakdown activities, see Morris and Burgoyne (1973).

[7] For a discussion of both the opportunities and problems presented by a matrix form of organization, see Argyris (1967), Wilemon and Gemmill (1971), Kingdon (1973), and Knight (1976).

degree of speciality is appropriate to its circumstances, what type of speciality, and the appropriate matching of manpower resources in terms of numbers, expertise, position in the formal hierarchy and location, whether in plant, divisional or Head Office.

Thus, for example, the organization represented in Fig. 6.2, and characterized by a role culture, may require a specialist personnel department whose strength lies mainly in its supplying a comprehensive range of substantive expertise and skills in designing and maintaining a service principally orientated towards steady-state personnel activities (e.g., well-administered and regularly monitored formalized systems and procedures, managed in the style of the 'conformist innovator'). Alternatively, an organization that is characterized by the frequency with which it has to cope with breakdown and crises may require a personnel department that is skilled in innovatory organizational design and perhaps prepared to consider the approach of the 'deviant innovator'. One thing is clear, though, the precise design of any personnel department must take account of three major factors: the dominant culture of the organization in which it is to operate (which will influence the style of operation), the model of the factors which determine this organizational context (which will suggest in which directions the personnel department may, in the future, have to change and develop), and the extent to which both suggest that the organization is more or less differentiated. For an organization that is highly differentiated, assuming that such a level of differentiation constitutes the appropriate response to challenges presented by the environment (Lawrence and Lorsch, 1967a), must require a specialist personnel function that, similarly, can provide the requisite level of differentiation.

A specialist personnel department faces the problem of differentiation in yet another respect. As was apparent in the discussion in chapter 2, the tasks a personnel department may undertake in relation to other parts of the organization combine several managerial functions, namely:

Executing (e.g., negotiating, counselling)
Servicing (e.g., canteens, recruitment, training)
Auditing (e.g., appraisal schemes, review of salary grades)
Advising (e.g., on organizational design, training and development opportunities)
Co-ordinating (e.g., career development opportunities, succession plans, fringe benefits) (Handy, 1976, page 273).

The problem is that, although performed by the same department, these activities can be in conflict and, as such, enhance the ambiguity that already surrounds the personnel function. This is particularly so if the same individual is expected to frequently combine incompatible positions. For example, as Handy comments 'the advisor who is also the auditor carries a sting in his relationship which is recognized and can be resented by the other party' (1976, page 273). Similarly, the position is difficult for the specialist who is asked to provide a service, which, in the role of advisor, he has already suggested is inappropriate or unnecessary.

Some of these problems may be alleviated if the roles in a specialist department are differentiated, to some extent, according to which managerial function (as well as specialism) is to be performed. Thus, some roles might be chiefly concerned with auditing and co-ordinating activities, some with advising, and some with servicing and executing. At the very least, attempts should be made to avoid combining in one role major incompatibilities. While the style of the 'conformist' innovator is likely to be particularly appropriate in carrying out auditing and co-ordinating activities, that of the 'deviant innovator' may more usefully match certain advisory and service relationships.

At first sight it might appear that the levels of differentiation suggested here (i.e., in terms of substantive content, processual skills, and managerial function) are impractical for two main reasons, namely costs in manpower resources, and the subsequent problems of integrating such a highly differentiated department. These criticisms may be considered in turn.

First, how costly would it be to organize a personnel department in the manner outlined here? It should be stressed that while the framework presented aims to lay out the range of *logical* possibilities, in practice the majority of organizations may be characterized in terms of one or two of the activity patterns (e.g., steady-state and breakdown), and by a prevailing culture. In practice, this is likely to determine where the bulk of a department's resources will have to be allocated, although it is hoped a totally reactive, rather than proactive, approach to existing organizational circumstances may be avoided. In situations of scarce resources, then, it is realistic for the personnel department to concentrate on developing a simplified matrix of roles, guided by which type of activity predominates throughout the organization (usually steady-state, with a subsidiary emphasis on either breakdown or on innovation). Within these constraints, the roles designed can aim at clustering characteristics that are logically compatible. For example, steady-state, auditing activities in, say, salary administration and management appraisal, may be undertaken by a 'conformist innovator', who may also be responsible for developing manpower planning systems. Or innovatory, advisory activities, in, say, management and organizational development, may be undertaken by a 'deviant innovator', who may also be responsible for re-examining some of the existing welfare services. Or breakdown/crises activities in industrial relations may be handled by a trouble-shooter, combining aspects from both the 'conformist' and 'deviant' innovator's approach, on a pragmatic basis, as he executes organizational policy in negotiating situations. Further, the matrix principle may be fully developed and implemented at some levels in the organization where many specialist roles already exist (e.g., divisional and Headquarters level), but used only in a rudimentary form at plant level.

At the same time, though, the approach outlined here may be used to evaluate which new roles should be developed in the future, or at present be given further resources. In other words, it may be used to establish priorities in the development as well as the initial design of the department, and to provide reasoned justifications for additional resources.

The integration of a highly differentiated management function is clearly of vital importance. Without it, not only may specialist activities 'go off at a tangent' and lose sight of overall objectives, but a lack of co-ordination between related activities may at best lead to the benefits of specialization being under-utilized, and at worst, provoke dysfunctional side effects. As it is, the problem of integration both within conventionally structured departments operating at the one level in the organization, and between departments at different levels (e.g., between divisional and plant level departments), often exists. Indeed, it was frequently commented upon by personnel specialists and line managers alike in the case-study organizations, particularly in the larger organizations and those in which there was a high degree of geographical and/or product diversity.

Although the matrix framework offered here as a basis on which to organize the personnel function can involve a high level role differentiation (if the organization has the resources and considers it appropriate to carry differentiation to its logical conclusion), it also suggests the basis on which integration can take place. That is, through the development of problem/task oriented project teams. For example, suppose the organization is confronted by a problem of labour shortage in several of its plants. In terms of substantive expertise, such a problem is likely to have implications for specialists in manpower planning, recruitment and selection, training, and wage and salary administration. It may ultimately involve industrial relations issues. At the same time, it will call upon the skills of specialists in handling steady-state and breakdown activities, and possibly policy-making and innovation. To cope with such a problem, then, the membership of the project team needs to be selected with a mix of these skills and, preferably, with the relevant substantive expertise matched with the processual skill appropriate to the problem in hand, in the one individual. Thus, the sort of team that might tackle the problem of severe labour shortages (if the function was highly differentiated) might comprise a manpower planning/steady-state activities specialist, a training/innovatory activities specialist, a recruitment/selection/breakdown and crises activities specialist and, additionally, a specialist in policy-making relating to wage and salary administration. Further, to provide co-ordination between plant, divisional and headquarters levels in the organization, ideally specialists may be drawn from at least two of these levels. For example, the manpower planner may come from the divisional level, the recruitment and training specialist from one of the relevant plants, and the wage and salary administrator be drawn from a policy-making group at headquarters. In addition, of course, the line management involved with

132

this problem in all the plants will also need to provide members of the project team.

Integration between project teams might be provided by the involvement of all members of the personnel department, at all levels, in a range of project teams, so that each has cross-cutting ties with other teams and problems.

If such an arrangement might provide the basic framework for an integrated approach to personnel management problem-solution, while fully exploiting the benefits of differentiation, its translation into a vehicle for effective decision-making and implementation will depend largely on the ability of the project team leaders to act as integrators both within and between project teams. Fortunately, research has provided many clues as to the characteristics of an effective integrator and the approach he should take. For example, we know from Lawrence and Lorsch's (1967b) work that tested expert power is the preferred power base for integrators, but that their rank and position in the organization must be high enough to allow them access to information, and resources sufficient to implement the decisions arrived at, quite apart from sufficient status to play an ambassadorial role in liaising with other project teams. Moreover, when conflicts do occur, it has been found that an approach which deals with them in a collaborative, problem-solving way, rather than by win-lose confrontations, is the more effective. Hence, the individuals appropriate to such a role should ideally possess the following characteristics:

... Be expert in more than one field of the organization's (function's) work
... Be able to handle role ambiguity, incompatibility and conflict without letting the role pressure turn into strain
... Have good interpersonal skills
... Be highly committed to the organization ... (Handy, 1976, page 305).

To a large extent, this could also serve as a description of the personal characteristics required to be an effective personnel manager. Faced as he is with the ambiguities that, at present, often surround his role, and with the tensions inherent in the function of a walking conflict resolution mechanism and mediator between different interest groups that is often attributed to him, the personnel manager requires a strong self-image and self-esteem to withstand the inevitable stresses of such a position. One way of alleviating them, though, is to apply the techniques of the organizational diagnostician to his own role, and with a realistic analysis of the opportunities and constraints facing personnel specialists within his own organizational context, choose an innovatory strategy appropriate to his own situation in the light of the objectives he wishes to achieve.

Appendix I

Some examples are given below of the many factors relevant to the operationalization of the six 'umbrella' variables employed in the general model of organizational context.

1. History and ownership

e.g., Age of organization
Growth pattern
Activity in acquisition/mergers
Changes in organization structure and top management
Changes in product line/service complexity
Changes in skill mix/demographic characteristics of employees
Extent and development of unionization in the organization
Pattern of industrial relations experience
(cf., Wasmuth, W. J., 1970)

e.g., Nationalized or private sector
Publicly quoted or private company
Structure and pattern of shareholding
Number and type of owners
(cf., Pugh *et al.*, 1963)

2. Size

eg., Average number of employees
Net assets
Market share
(cf., Pugh *et al.*, 1963)

3. Technology

e.g., Level of technical complexity in work processes
(cf., unit and small batch production/large batch, assembly and mass production/process production).
(Woodward, 1965)

e.g., Degree of routiness/non-routiness in work processes
(cf., variability of stimuli/degree to which search procedures are analysable)
(Perrow, 1967a, 1967b, 1970a)

e.g., Degree of integration in work processes
(cf., pooled/sequential/reciprocal interdependence)
(Thompson, J.D., 1967)

4. Goals and objectives

e.g., Societal goals
Output goals
System goals
Product goals
Derived goals

e.g., Organizational success criteria

Official goals
Operative goals
(Perrow, 1970a)

5. Environment

e.g., Economic environment
Market environments (e.g., product market, including customers'
requirements and strategies of competitors, levels of uncertainty in both).
(e.g., labour market, including number and availability of potential
employees, strategies of competitors to attract this labour).
Scientific knowledge environment
Political/legislative environment
Societal/cultural environment

All such environments may be further characterized in terms of how they
are perceived to operate:

e.g., in terms of their degree of uncertainty (Lawrence and Lorsch, 1967a).
e.g., in terms of their degree of turbulence (Emery and Trist, 1965).
cf., for example, the characterization of the organizational task environment in
terms of:
Complexity (i.e., the number of external factors which an organization has to
control).
Diversity (i.e., the extent to which the external factors are different from each
other as to the nature of the problems that they pose for the organization).
Instability (i.e., the rapidity with which external factors change over time).
Uncertainty (i.e., the extent to which (a) the occurrence of external factors can
be predicted, and (b) the nature of the problem or content of the event can
be predicted).
Hostility (i.e., extent to which the external factors pose a threat to the
organization's goals and objectives).
Dependence (i.e., the extent to which the external factors are essential to the
organization's goal achievement, taking into account the availability of
alternative sources of supplies and/or purchasers. (Shortell, 1977).

6. Employees

e.g., Demographic characteristics (age, sex, ethnic group)
Job expectations and preferences
Job experience (e.g., skills and work practices acquired) (cf., Gowler and
Legge, 1972).
Labour costs

Conclusions

The mention of resources at the end of the last chapter brings us back to the central dilemma confronted, if not fully resolved, by this essay. For, if the personnel function (in its broadest sense) is to achieve in practice the predominance it is accorded in theory, the relationship between personnel management and the achievement of organizational success criteria must be clearly demonstrated, in unequivocal terms. This task is difficult enough even in those organizations whose focal task concerns the development of satisfying personal relationships as ends in themselves (cf., Abrams and McCulloch, 1976). But in cost-conscious and commercial organizations in a capitalist society, when such a demonstration tends to be equated with quantifiable and financial results, the task is doubly difficult. A specialist personnel department has a key role to play here: not only in turning theory into fact (i.e., by using its expertise to develop strategies and establish guidelines to facilitate appropriate human resource utilization throughout the organization), but in demonstrating both *how* and, in spite of the difficulties involved, the *extent*, 'good' personnel management can and does contribute to organizational success. Yet, to obtain adequate resources to undertake these tasks, a personnel department requires power which, at present, in many organizations it lacks, precisely because of its inability to convince those who do control resources of its potential contribution. It is the old chicken and egg situation. Until personnel can demonstrate its contribution to organizational success, it will be unable to generate adequate resources for its work, but until it does so, it will be unable to achieve this potential contribution.

How can personnel management and, in particular, personnel specialists, break out of this vicious circle? In this essay, a contingent approach both to substantive issues of personnel management, and to the design and operating style of its institutionalized presence, the personnel department, has been suggested as one way out. It is hoped that just as a vicious circle can accelerate deterioratively into a regressive spiral, so in this way, and reinforced by environmental change, a *progressive* spiral may be and, hopefully, is being, initiated.

References

ABRAMS, P. and MCCULLOCH, A., *Communes, Sociology and Society*, Cambridge: Cambridge University Press, 1976.

AIC Management Consultants, *Survey of Executive Salaries and Fringe Benefits*, London: AIC, 1970, 1971, 1972.

AITKEN, O., 'Equal pay's early days', *Personnel Management*, **8**, 7, July 1976, p. 40.

ALLEN, V. L., *Social Analysis*, London: Longman, 1975.

ANSOFF, I., *Corporate Strategy*, New York: McGraw-Hill, 1965.

ARGYRIS, C., 'Today's problems with tomorrow's organizations', *Journal of Management Studies*, **4**, 31–55, 1967.

BAILEY, F. G. (Ed.), *Debate and Compromise: The Politics of Innovation*, Oxford: Blackwell, 1973.

BAIN, G. S., *The Growth of White Collar Unionism*, Oxford: Oxford University Press, 1970.

BAMBER, G., 'Trade unions for managers?' *Personnel Review*, **5**, 4, 36–41, 1976.

BARBER, B., 'Some problems in the sociology of professions,' *Daedalus*, **92**, 1963.

BARTHOLOMEW, D. J., *Stochastic Models for Social Processes*, New York: Wiley, 1967.

BARTHOLOMEW, D. J. (Ed.), *Manpower Planning, Selected Readings*, Harmondsworth: Penguin, 1976.

BARTHOLOMEW, D. J. and MORRIS, B. R. (Eds.), *Aspects of Manpower Planning*, London: English Universities Press, 1971.

BECKER, S. W. and NEUHAUSER, D., *The Efficient Organization*, New York: Elsevier, 1975.

BEER, S., *The Organization of the Manchester Business School from 1970*, Manchester: Manchester Business School, 1970.

BEER, S., *Brain of The Firm: The Managerial Cybernetics of Organization*, London: Allen Lane, 1972.

BENNIS, W. G. *et al.*, *The Planning of Change*, New York: Holt, Rinehart and Winston, 1969.

BLAU, P. M., *Exchange and Power in Social Life*, New York: Wiley, 1964.

BOWEY, A. M., *The Sociology of Organisations*, London: Hodder and Stoughton, 1976.

BOWEY, A. M. and LUPTON, T., 'Productivity drift and the structure of the pay packet', *Journal of Management Studies*, **7**, 156–171, 310–334, 1970.

BOWLEY, A., *Salary Structures for Management Careers*, London: IPM, 1971.

BROWN, A., 'The overtime coin—management and labour motivation, *Management Decision*, **3**, 4, 26–30, 1969.

BRUMMET, R. E. LEE, FLAMHOLTZ, E. G. and PYLE, W. C., 'Human resource measurement—A challenge for accountants, *Accounting Review*, **13**, 217–224, 1968.

BRUMMET, R. E. LEE, FLAMHOLTZ, E. G. and PYLE, W. C., *Human Resource Accounting: Development and Implementation in Industry*, Ann Arbor: Foundation for Research on Human Behavior, 1969.

BRYAN, S. E., 'The total management concept', *Business Topics*, Spring 1966.

BUCKINGHAM, G. L., *What to do about Equal Pay for Women*, Epping: Gower Press, 1974.

BUCKLEY, J. E., 'Equal pay in America'. *In* Pettman, B. O. (Ed.), *Equal Pay for Women*, Bradford: MCB Books, 1975.

BURNS, T. and STALKER, G. M., *The Management of Innovation*, London: Tavistock, 1961.

BUTTERISS, M., *Job Enrichment and Employee Participation: A Study*, London: IPM, 1971.

CAIRNCROSS, F., 'Why so few recruits?' *Guardian*, 21 July, 1976.

CANNON, J. A., 'Human resource accounting—a critical comment', *Personnel Review*, **3**, 3, 14–20, 1974a.

CANNON, J. A., 'A further comment on human resource accounting', *Personnel Review*, **3**, 4, 38–42, 1974b.

CARR SAUNDERS, A. M. and WILSON, P. A., *The Professions*, Oxford: Oxford University Press, 1933.

CARTWRIGHT, D., 'Influence, leadership, control'. *In* March, J. G. (Ed.), *Handbook of Organizations*, Chicago: Rand McNally, 1965.

CHAYES, A. H., 'Make your Equal Opportunity Program court proof', *Harvard Business Review*, **52**, 5, 81–89, 1974.

CHEEK, L. M., 'Cost effectiveness comes to the personnel function', *Harvard Business Review*, **50**, 3, 96–105, 1972.

CHILD, J., 'Organizational Structure, environment and performance: the role of strategic choice', *Sociology*, **6**, 1–22, 1972.

CHILD, J. and MANSFIELD, R. M., 'Technology, size, and organization structure', *Sociology*, **6**, 369–393, 1972.

CHURCHILL, N. C. and SHANK, J. K., 'Affirmative action and guilt-edged goals', *Harvard Business Review*, **54**, 2, 111–116, 1976.

C.I.R., *BSR Limited*, Report No. 5, Cmnd 4274, London: HMSO, 1970.

C.I.R., *Armstrong Patents Company Limited*, Report No. 13, Cmnd 4541, London: HMSO, 1970.

C.I.R., *Clayton Dewandre Company Limited*, Report No. 15, Cmnd 4640, London: HMSO, 1971.

C.I.R., *The Role of Management in Industrial Relations*, Report No. 34, London: HMSO, 1973.

GLEGG, S., *Power, Rule and Domination*, London: Routledge and Kegan Paul, 1975.

COMMISSION OF EUROPEAN COMMUNITIES, *Statute for European Companies: Amended Proposal for a Regulation. In Bulletin of the European Communities Supplement*, April 1975.

CONFEDERATION OF BRITISH INDUSTRY, *The Responsibilities of the British Public Company. Final Report of the Company Affairs Committee*, London: CBI, 1973.

COOK, A. H., 'Equal pay: where is it?' *Industrial Relations*, **14**, 158–177, 1975.

COURTIS, J., 'Employees are not always an asset', *Accountant's Weekly*, 5 January 1973.

COWAN, N., 'New rights for the redundant', *Personnel Management*, **7**, 10, 28–32, 1975.

CRAFT, J. A. and BIRNBERG, J. G., 'Human resource accounting: perspective and prospects', *Industrial Relations, A Journal of Economy and Society*, **15**, 2–12, 1976.

CRENSON, M. A., *The Un-Politics of Air Pollution: A Study of Non Decision-Making in the Cities*, Baltimore: John Hopkins, 1971.

CRICHTON, A., *Personnel Management in Context*, London: Batsford, 1968.

CROZIER, M., *The Bureaucratic Phenomenon*, London: Tavistock, 1964.

CUMING, M. W., *The Theory and Practice of Personnel Management*, (Third Edn.), London: Heinemann, 1975.

CYERT, R. M. and MARCH, J. G., *A Behavioral Theory of the Firm*, Englewood Cliffs, N. J.: Prentice-Hall, 1963.

DAHL, R. A., 'The concept of power', *Behavioral Science*, **2**, 201–215, 1957.

DALTON, G. W. *et al.*, *Organizational Change and Development*, Homewood, Illinois: Irwin-Dorsey, 1970.

DANIEL, W. W., 'The high price of redundancy payments', *Personnel Management*, **8**, 9, 16–18, 1976.

DANIELS, A. K., 'Professionalism in formal organizations'. *In* McKinlay, J. B. (Ed.), *Processing People, Cases in Organizational Behaviour*, London: Holt, Rinehart and Winston, 1975.

DAVIS, L. E. and CHERNS, A. B. (Eds.), *The Quality of Working Life*, Vols. I and II, New York: The Free Press, 1975.

DEPARTMENT OF TRADE, *Report of the Committee of Inquiry on Industrial Democracy (The Bullock Report)*, Cmnd 6706, London: HMSO, 1977.

138

DOERINGER, P. B. and PIORE, M. J., *Internal Labor Markets and Manpower Analysis*, Lexington, Mass: Heath, 1971.

DONALDSON, J. and GOWLER, D., 'Prerogatives, participation and managerial stress', *In* Gowler, D. and Legge, K. (Eds.), *Managerial Stress*, Epping: Gower Press, 102–114, 1975.

DONALDSON, L., 'Woodward, technology, organizational structure and performance—a critique of the universal generalization', *Journal of Management Studies*, **13**, 255–73, 1976.

DRUCKER, P., *The Practice of Management*, Mercury Books, London, 1961. First published 1954.

DUBIN, R., 'Power, function, and organization', *Pacific Sociological Review*, **6**, 16–24, 1963.

ECCLES, A. J., 'Sit-ins, worker co-operatives and some implications for organization', *Personnel Review*, **6**, 2, 39–44, 1977.

EDWARDS, W., 'Utility, subjective probability, their interaction and variance preferences', *Journal of Conflict Resolution*, **6**, 42–51, 1962.

EMERSON, R. E., 'Power-dependence relations', *American Sociological Review*, **27**, 31–41, 1962.

EMERY, F. E. (Ed.), *Systems Thinking*, Harmondsworth: Penguin, 1969.

EMERY, F. E. and TRIST, E. L., 'The causal texture of organizational environments', *Human Relations*, **8**, 21–32, 1965.

ENGINEERING INDUSTRY TRAINING BOARD, *Training Officers in the Engineering Industry*, London: EITB, 1974.

EPSTEIN, E. M., 'The social role of business enterprise in Britain: An American perspective: Part II', *Journal of Management Studies*, **14**, 281–316, 1977.

ETZIONI, A., *Modern Organizations*, Englewood Cliffs, N.J.: Prentice Hall, 1964.

FISCHER, F. E., 'The personnel function in tomorrow's company', *Personnel*, **45**, 64–71, 1968.

FLAMHOLTZ, E., 'A model of human resource valuation: A stochastic process with service rewards', *Accounting Review*, **46**, 253–267, 1971.

FLAMHOLTZ, E., 'Human resource accounting: measuring positional replacement costs', *Human Resource Management*, 8–16, Spring 1973.

FLAMHOLTZ, E., 'Human resource accounting: a review of theory and research', *Journal of Management Studies*, **11**, 44–61, 1974.

FLANDERS, A., *The Fawley Productivity Agreements*, London: Faber and Faber, 1964.

FLANDERS, H., 'The AT and T company manpower laboratory, circa 1971', *Academy of Management Proceedings*, 31st Annual Meeting, 203–206, August 1971.

FOGARTY, M., *Company Responsibility and Participation: A New Agenda*, Broadsheet No. 554, London: PEP, August 1975.

FOULKES, F. K., 'The expanding role of the personnel function', *Harvard Business Review*, **53**, 2, 71–84, 1975.

FOULKES, F. K. and MORGAN, H. M., 'Organizing and staffing the personnel function', *Harvard Business Review*, **55**, 3, 142–154, 1977.

FOX, A., 'Industrial sociology and industrial relations', *Research Paper No 3*, Royal Commission on Trades Unions and Employers' Associations, London: HMSO, 1966a.

FOX, A., *Time-Span of Discretion Theory: An Appraisal*, London: IPM, 1966b.

FREIDSON, E., 'The impurity of professional authority'. *In* Becker, H. S., Geer, B., Riesman, D. and Weiss, R. S. (Eds.), *Institutions and the Person*, Chicago: Aldine, 1968.

FRENCH, WENDELL, 'Organization development: objectives, assumptions and strategies', *California Management Review*, **XII**, 2, 23–34, 1969.

FRENCH, WENDELL and HENNING, DALE, 'The authority-influence role of the functional specialist in management', *Academy of Management Journal*, **9**, 187–203, 1966.

FRENCH, J. R. P. and RAVEN, B., 'The bases of social power'. *In* Cartwright, D., and Zander, A. F. (Eds.), *Group Dynamics*, (Second Edn), Evanston, Ill.: Row, Petersen and Co., 1960.

FRIEDLANDER, F. and BROWN, D. L., 'Organization development', *Research Paper*, 1974.

FRIEDMANN, J., 'A response to Altshuler: comprehensive planning as a process', *Journal of the American Institute of Planners*, **31**, August 1965.

139

GENNARD, J. and LASKO, R., 'The individual and the strike', *British Journal of Industrial Relations*, **13**, 346–370, 1975.

GILES, W. J. and ROBINSON, D. F., *Human Asset Accounting*, London: IPM and ICMA, 1972.

GILL, D., UNGERSON, B. and THAKUR, M., *Performance Appraisal in Perspective*, London: IPM, 1973.

GILLESPIE, A., 'Personnel management—dominant ideas', *Personnel Review*, **2**, 1, 62–64, 1973a.

GILLESPIE, A., *The Management of Wage Payment Systems*, London: Kogan Page, 1973b.

GLOVER, I., 'Why do we train our top men to be second best?', *Guardian*, 4 February, 1976, p. 16.

GLUCKMAN, M., *Custom and Conflict in Africa*, Oxford: Blackwell, 1956.

GLUECK, W. F., *Personnel, a Diagnostic Approach*, Dallas, Texas: Business Publications, 1974.

GOFFMAN, E., *The Presentation of Self in Everyday Life*, Harmondsworth: Penguin, 1969.

GORDON, G., MacEACHRON, A. E. and FISHER, G. L., 'A contingency model for the design of problem solving research: A perspective on diffusion research', *Health and Society*, Spring 1974.

GORFIN, C. C., 'The suggestion scheme: a contribution to morale or an economic transaction?' *British Journal of Industrial Relations*, **7**, 368–384, 1969.

GOWER, L. C. B., *The Principles of Modern Company Law*, (3rd Edn.), London: Stevens and Sons, 1969.

GOWLER, D., 'Determinants of the supply of labour to the firm', *Journal of Management Studies*, **6**, 73–95, 1969.

GOWLER, D., 'Values, contracts and job satisfaction', *Personnel Review*, **3**, 4, 4–14, 1974.

GOWLER, D. and LEGGE, K., 'Occupational role development: Part I' *Personnel Review*, **2**, 2, 12–27, 1972.

GOWLER, D. and LEGGE, K., 'Perceptions and the principle of cumulation', *In* Warner, M. (Ed.), *The Sociology of the Workplace*, London: George Allen and Unwin, 1973a.

GOWLER, D. and LEGGE, K., *Final Report on the Organization of Local Marriage Guidance Councils*, Rugby: NMGC, 1973b.

GREENLAW, P. S. and SMITH, R. D., *Personnel Management: a Management Science Approach*, Scranton, Penn: International Textbooks, 1970.

GREENWOOD, E., 'Attributes of a profession', *Social Work*, **2**, 45–55, July 1957.

GREINER, L. E., 'Patterns of organizational change', *Harvard Business Review*, **45**, 3, 119–130, 1967.

HANDY, C. B., *Understanding Organizations*, Harmondsworth: Penguin, 1976.

HARRISON, R., 'Understanding your organization's character', *Harvard Business Review*, **50**, 3, 119–128, 1972.

HEALTH AND SAFETY AT WORK ACT, London: HMSO, 1974.

HEKIMIAN, J. S. and JONES, G. H., 'Put people on your balance sheet', *Harvard Business Review*, **45**, 1, 105–113, 1967.

HERMAN, S. M., *The People Specialists*, New York: Knopf, 1968.

HERMANSON, R. H., 'Accounting for human assets', *Occasional Paper No. 14*, East Lancing, Michigan: Bureau of Business and Economic Research, 1964.

HICKSON, D. J., PUGH, D. S. and PHEYSEY, D. C., 'Operations technology and organization structure: an empirical reappraisal', *Administrative Science Quarterly*, **14**, 378–397, 1969.

HICKSON, D. J., HININGS, C. R., LEE, G. A., SCHNECK, R. E. and PENNINGS, J. M., 'A "strategic contingencies" theory of intra organizational power', *Administrative Science Quarterly*, **16**, 216–229, 1971.

HILL, P., *Towards a New Philosophy of Management: the Company Development of Shell UK Ltd.*, London: Gower Press, 1971.

HONEY, P., 'On the trail of the personnel professional', *Personnel Management*, **8**, 4, 33–35, 1976.

HUGHES, E., *Men and Their Work*, Glencoe, Ill.: Free Press, 1958.

HUGHES, E., *The Sociological Eye*, Chicago: Aldine-Atherton, 1971.

INBUCON/AIC Management Consultants Ltd., *Survey of Executive Salaries and Fringe Benefits'*, 1975, 1976.

IPM, 'Statement on personnel management and personnel policies', *Personnel Management*, March 1963.

JACKSON, J. A. (Ed.), *Professions and Professionalization*, Sociological Studies 3, Cambridge: Cambridge University Press, 1970.

JAQUES, E., *Equitable Payment*, London: Heinemann Educational Books, 1961.

JAQUES, E., *Time-Span Handbook*, London, Heinemann, 1964.

JENKINS, C., 'Is personnel still underpowered?', *Personnel Management*, **5**, 6, 34–35, 1973.

JOHNSON, T. J., *Professions and Power*, London: MacMillan, 1972.

JUCIUS, M. J., *Personnel Management*, (Eighth Edn.), Homewood, Illinois: Irwin, 1975.

KAPFERER, B., *Urban Africans at Work*, Unpublished PhD Thesis, Department of Social Anthropology, University of Manchester, 1969.

KATZ, D. and KHAN, R. L., *The Social Psychology of Organizations*, New York: Wiley, 1966.

KEENAY, G. A., *Manpower Planning in Large Organizations: a Statistical Approach*, Doctoral Thesis, University of Cambridge, 1973.

KESSLER, S. and PALMER, G., 'Reconsidering recognition', *Personnel Management*, **7**, 7, 18–21, 1975.

KHAN, R. L., WOLFE, D. M., QUINN, R. P., SNOEK, J. D. and ROSENTHAL, R. A., *Organizational Stress*, New York: Wiley, 1964.

KINGDON, D. R., *Matrix Organization*, London: Tavistock, 1973.

KLEIN, L., *A Social Scientist in Industry*, Epping: Gower Press, 1976.

KNIGHT, K., 'Matrix organization—a review', *Journal of Management Studies*, **13**, 2, 111–130, 1976.

LAWRENCE, P. R. and LORSCH, J. W., *Organization and Environment*, Cambridge, Mass.: Harvard University Press, 1967a.

LAWRENCE, P. R. and LORSCH, J. W., 'New management job: the integrator', *Harvard Business Review*, **45**, 6, 142–151, 1967b.

LEE, R. A. and YOUNG, W. McEWAN, 'A contingency approach to work week restructuring', *Personnel Review*, **6**, 2, 45–55, 1977.

LEGGE, K., 'The operation of the "regressive spiral" in the labour market', *Journal of Management Studies*, **7**, 1–22, 1970.

LEGGE, K., 'Flexible working hours—panacea or placebo?', *Management Decision*, **12**, 264–280, 1974.

LEGGE, K. and EXLEY, M., 'Authority, ambiguity and adaptation: the personnel specialist's dilemma', *Industrial Relations Journal*, **6**, 3, 51–65, 1975.

LEV, B. and SCHWARTZ, A., 'On the use of the economic concept of human capital in financial statements', *Accounting Review*, **46**, 1, 103–112, 1971.

LEV, B. and SCHWARTZ, A., 'On the use of human capital in financial statements: a reply', *Accounting Review*, **47**, 1, 153–154, 1972.

LIKERT, R., *The Human Organization: its Management and Value*, New York: McGraw-Hill, 1967.

LINDBLOM, C. E., 'The science of "muddling through"', *Public Administration Review*, Spring 1959.

LINKLATER, P. S., 'Manpower planning in an industrial company—some experience', *In* Lawrence, J. (Ed.), *Company Manpower Planning in Perspective*, London: IPM, 1975.

LUKES, S., *Power, a Radical View*, London: MacMillan, 1974.

LUPTON, T., *Industrial Behaviour and Personnel Management*, London: IPM, 1964.

LUPTON, T., *Management and the Social Sciences*, (Second Edn), London: Lyon, Grant, and Green, 1970. First published 1966.

LUPTON, T., 'Structure, process and stress'. *In* Gowler, D. and Legge, K. (Eds.), *Managerial Stress*, Epping: Gower Press, 1975a.

LUPTON, T., "Best fit" in the design of organizations', *Personnel Review*, **4**, 1, 15–31, 1975b.

LUPTON, T. and GOWLER, D., 'Selecting a wage payment system', *Research Paper No. 3*, London: Engineering Employers' Federation, 1969.

LUPTON, T. and GOWLER, D., 'Wage payment systems: a review of current thinking', *Personnel Management*, **4**, 11, 1972.

LUSSATO, B., *A Critical Introduction to Organization Theory*, London: MacMillan, 1976, translated by Alison R. Julier. (First published by Dunod, Paris, 1972).

LYONS, T. P., *The Personnel Function in a Changing Environment*, London: Pitman, 1971.

141

MACE, J. D. and WILKINSON, G. C. G., 'Are labour markets competitive? A case study of engineers', *British Journal of Industrial Relations*, **XV**, 1–17, 1977.

MACKAY, D. I. et al., *Labour Markets under Different Employment Conditions*, London: George Allen and Unwin, 1971.

MARGERISON, C. J., 'Personnel management within the employees' organization', *Personnel Review*, **5**, 2, 41–44, 1976a.

MARGERISON, C. J., 'A constructive approach to appraisal', *Personnel Management*, **8**, 7, 30–33, 1976b.

MARGULIES, N. and RAIA, A. P., *Organizational Development, Values, Process, and Technology*, New York: McGraw-Hill, 1972.

MARSH, A. I., 'The staffing of industrial relations management in the engineering industry', *Industrial Relations Journal*, **2**, 2, 14–23, 1971.

MARTIN, R. and FRYER, R. H., *Redundancy and Paternalist Capitalism*, London: George Allen and Unwin, 1973.

MCBEATH, G., *Management Remuneration Policy*, London: Business Books, 1969.

MCBEATH, G. and RANDS, D. N., *Salary Administration*, London: Business Books, 1969.

MCCAIG, P., 'Too academic', in 'Letters', *Personnel Management*, **8**, 9, 44, 1976.

MCFARLAND, D. E., *Company Officers Assess the Personnel Function*, AMA Research Report No 79, New York: American Management Association, 1967.

MCFARLAND, D. E., *Personnel Management: Theory and Practice*, New York: MacMillan, 1968.

MECHANIC, D., 'Sources of power of lower participants in complex organizations', *Administrative Science Quarterly*, **7**, 349–364, 1962.

MEGGINSON, L. C., *Personnel—A Behavioral Approach to Administration*, (Revised Edn), Homewood, Illinois: Irwin, 1972.

MEPHAM, G. J., *Equal Opportunity and Equal Pay*, London: IPM, 1974.

MERTON, R. K., *Social Theory and Social Structure*, Glencoe, Ill.: The Free Press, 1957.

MEYER, H., KAY, E. and FRENCH, F., 'Split roles in performance appraisal', *Harvard Business Review*, **43**, 123–129, 1965.

MILLER, F. B., 'The personnel dilemma: profession or not', *Personnel Journal*, **38**, 53–56, 1959.

MILLERSON, G., *The Qualifying Associations: a Study in Professionalisation*, London: Routledge and Kegan Paul, 1964.

MILLS, A. J., 'Worker "sit-ins"', *Personnel Review*, **5**, 4, 46–50, 1976.

MILLS, C. W., *White Collar: the American Middle Classes*, New York: Oxford University Press, 1951.

MINER, J. B., 'Levels of motivation to manage among personnel and industrial relations managers', *Journal of Applied Psychology*, **61**, 419–427, 1976.

MINER, J. B. and MINER, M. G., *Personnel and Industrial Relations, a Managerial Approach*, (Second Edn), New York: MacMillan, 1973.

MITCHELL, G. D. (Ed.), *A Dictionary of Sociology*, London: Routledge and Kegan Paul, 1968.

MOLANDER, C. F., 'Management by objectives in perspective', *Journal of Management Studies*, **9**, 74–81, 1972.

MORRIS, J., 'Three aspects of the person in social life'. *In* Ruddock, R. (Ed.), *Six Approaches to the Person*, London: Routledge and Kegan Paul, 1972.

MORRIS, J. and BURGOYNE, J. G., *Developing Resourceful Managers*, London: IPM, 1973.

MORSE, J. J. and LORSCH, J. W., 'Beyond theory Y', *Harvard Business Review*, **48**, 3, 61–68, 1970.

MUMFORD, E., 'Job satisfaction: A method of analysis', *Personnel Review*, **1**, 2, 48–57, 1972a.

MUMFORD, E., *Job Satisfaction. A Study of Computer Specialists*, London: Longman, 1972b.

MUMFORD, E., 'A strategy for the redesign of work', *Personnel Review*, **5**, 2, 33–39, 1976.

MUMFORD, P., *Redundancy and Security of Employment*, Epping: Gower Press, 1975.

MYERS, C. A., 'The changing role of the personnel manager', *Personnel Review*, **1**, 1, 6–20, 1971.

MYERS, S., *Managing Without Unions*, Reading, Mass.: Addison-Wesley, 1976.

NAGEL, J. H., *The Descriptive Analysis of Power*, New Haven, Conn.: Yale University Press, 1975.

NEWBOULD, G. D., WILSON, K. W. and STRAY, S. J., 'Academic salaries—A personal application of managerial economics', *Journal of Management Studies*, **13**, 175–182, 1976.

OWEN, T., 'Getting the best out of Europe', *Personnel Management*, **8**, 2, 16–20, 1976.

PATERSON, T. T., *Job Evaluation: Vol. 1. A New Method*, London: Business Books, 1972.

PATERSON, T. T., *Job Evaluation: Vol. 2. A Manual for the Paterson Method*, London: Business Books, 1972.

PAUL, W. J. and ROBERTSON, K. B., *Job Enrichment and Employee Motivation*, Epping: Gower Press, 1970.

PAYNE, R. and PUGH, D. S., 'Organizational structure and climate'. In Dunnette, M. D. (Ed.), *Handbook of Industrial and Organizational Psychology*, New York: Rand McNally, 1976.

THE PENGUIN ENGLISH DICTIONARY, Second Edition, Harmondsworth: Penguin, 1969.

PERROW, C., 'The analysis of goals in complex organizations', *American Sociological Review*, **26**, 854–866, 1961.

PERROW, C., 'A framework for the comparative analysis of organization', *American Sociological Review*, **32**, 194–208, 1967a.

PERROW, C., 'Technology and organizational structure'. In *Proceedings of the 19th Annual Meeting of the Industrial Relations Research Association*, Madison, Wis., 1967b.

PERROW, C., *Organizational Analysis*, London: Tavistock, 1970a.

PERROW, C., 'Departmental power and perspectives in industrial firms'. *In* Zald, M. N. (Ed.), *Power in Organizations*, Nashville, Tenn.: Vanderbilt University Press, 1970b.

PETTIGREW, A. M., 'Information control as a power resource', *Sociology* **6**, 187–204, 1972.

PETTIGREW, A. M., *The Politics of Organizational Decision-Making*, London: Tavistock 1973.

PETTIGREW, A. M., 'Towards a political theory of organizational intervention', *Human Relations*, **28**, 191–208, 1976.

PETTMAN, B. O. (Ed.), *Equal Pay for Women*, Bradford: MCB Books, 1975.

PIGORS, P. and MYERS, C. A., *Personnel Administration*, (Sixth Edn), New York: McGraw-Hill, 1969.

POLSBY, N. W., *Community Power and Political Theory*, New Haven, Conn.: Yale University Press, 1963.

POOLE, M., 'A back seat for personnel', *Personnel Management*, **5**, 5, 38–41, 1973.

POOLE, M., 'A power analysis of workplace labour relations', *Industrial Relations Journal*, **7**, 3, 31–43, 1976.

PRENTICE, G., 'The training officer in search of influence', *Personnel Management*, **7**, 7, 26–29, 1975.

PRESSMAN, J. L. and WILDAVSKY, A. B., *Implementation*, Berkeley: University of California Press, 1973.

PUGH, D. S., HICKSON, D. J., HININGS, C. R., McDONALD, K., TURNER, C. and LUPTON, T. 'A conceptual scheme for organizational analysis', *Administrative Science Quarterly*, **8**, 275–294, 1963.

PUGH, D. S., HICKSON, D. J., HININGS, C. R. and TURNER, C., 'Dimensions of organization structure', *Administrative Science Quarterly*, **13**, 65–105, 1968.

PUGH, D. S., HICKSON, D. J., HININGS, C. R. and TURNER, C., 'The context of organization structures', *Administrative Science Quarterly*, **14**, 94–114, 1969.

PURCELL, T. V., 'How GE measures managers in Fair Employment', *Harvard Business Review*, **52**, 6, 99–104, 1974.

RAIA, A., 'Goal setting and self control', *Journal of Management Studies*, **2**, 34–53, 1965.

RAIA, A., 'A second look at management goals and controls', *California Management Review*, 49–58, Summer 1966.

RHODE, J. G., LAWLER III, E. E. and SUNDEM, G. L., 'Human resource accounting: a critical assessment', *Industrial Relations, A Journal of Economy and Society*, **15**, 13–25, 1976.

RICHARDSON, R., 'The personnel department and its business objectives', *Personnel*, **45**, 1, 41–45, 1968.

RITZER, G. and TRICE, H. M., *An Occupation in Conflict*, Ithica, N.Y.: Cornell University Press, 1969.

ROBINSON, D., 'Myths of the local labour market', *Personnel*, **1**, 1, 36–39, 1967.

ROBINSON, D., 'External and internal labour markets'. *In* Robinson D. (Ed.), *Local Labour Markets and Wage Structures*, Epping: Gower Press, 1970.

ROCK, M. L. (Ed.), *Handbook of Wage and Salary Administration*, New York: McGraw-Hill, 1972.

ROOTS, P. J., 'Keeping up with employee rights', *Personnel Management*, **7**, 9, 31–35, 1975.

RUBENSTEIN, M., *A Practical Guide to the Employment Protection Act*, London: IPM, 1975.

RUBENSTEIN, M. and FROST, Y., 'The Equal Pay Act—The EAT to the rescue', *Personnel Management*, **9**, 2, 6–9, 1977.

RUSHING, W. A., 'Hardness of material as related to a division of labor in manufacturing industries', *Administrative Science Quarterly*, **13**, 229–245, 1968.

SAYLES, L. R., *Behavior of Industrial Work Groups*, New York: Wiley, 1958.

SAYLES, L. R., *Managerial Behavior*, New York: McGraw-Hill, 1964.

SCOULLER, A., 'All you need to know about disclosure', *Personnel Management*, **7**, 8, 25–28, 1975.

SHANIN, T., 'Models and Thought'. *In* Shanin, T. (Ed.), *The Rules of the Game*, London: Tavistock, 1972.

SHORTELL, S. M., 'The role of environment in a configurational theory of organizations', *Human Relations*, **30**, 275–302, 1977.

SILVERMAN, D., *The Theory of Organisations*, London: Heinemann, 1970.

SIMON, H. A., 'On the concept of organizational goal'. *In* Hill, W. A. and Egan, D. (Eds.), *Readings in Organization Theory: a Behavioral Approach*, Boston, Mass: Allyn and Bacon, 1967.

SIMON, H. A., *Administrative Behavior*, (Third Edn.), New York: The Free Press, 1976. First published 1947.

SMITH, A. R. (Ed.), *Models of Manpower Systems*, London: English Universities Press, 1971.

SOFER, C., *The Organization From Within*, London: Tavistock, 1961.

SOFER, C., 'The assessment of organizational change' *Journal of Management Studies*, **1**, 128–142, 1964.

STAINER, G., *Manpower Planning*, London: Heinemann, 1971.

STEWART, A. and STEWART, V., *Tomorrow's Men Today*, London: IPM and Institute of Manpower Studies, 1976.

STEWART, M., *Employment Conditions in Europe*, (Second Edn), Epping: Gower Press, 1976.

STRAUSS, G., 'Introduction' (to a collection of papers on HRA) *Industrial Relations, A Journal of Economy and Society*, **15**, 1, 1976.

STRAUSS, G. and SAYLES, L. R., *Personnel, the Human Problems of Management*, Englewood Cliffs, N.J.: Prentice-Hall, 1960.

TANNENBAUM, R. and DAVIS, S. A., 'Values, man, and organization', *Industrial, Management Review*, **10**, 2, 67–86, Winter 1969.

TAYLOR, J., 'The human side of work: the sociological approach to work system design', *Personnel Review*, **4**, 3, 17–22, 1975.

THAKUR, M., *OD: The Search for Identity*, London: IPM, 1974.

THAKUR, M., *Manpower Planning in Action*, London: IPM, 1975.

THOMASON, G. F., *A Textbook of Personnel Management*, London: IPM, 1975. (Second Edn., 1976).

THOMPSON, J. D., *Organizations in Action*, New York: McGraw-Hill, 1967.

TOFFLER, A., *Future Stock*, London: Bodley Head, 1970.

'Top twenty firms taking no account of sex discrimination legislation', *Personnel Management*, **8**, 12, December 1976, p. 5.

TOSI, H. L. and CARROLL, S., 'Managerial reactions to management by objectives', *Academy of Management Journal*, 415–426, December 1968.

TOSI, H. L. and CARROLL, S., 'Some factors affecting the success of management by objectives', *Journal of Management Studies*, **7**, 209–223, 1970.

TOWLE, J. W., SCHOEN, S. H. and HILGERT, R. L., *Problems and Policies in Personnel Management: a Casebook*, (Second Edn), Boston: Houghton Mifflin, 1972.

TOYNE, P., 'The flight from the factory floor', *Sunday Times, Business News*, 3 October, 1976, p. 62.

TRIST, E. L., HIGGIN, G. W., MURRAY, H. and POLLOCK, A. B., *Organizational Choice*, London: Tavistock, 1963.

TURNER, H. A., CLACK, G. and ROBERTS, G. *Labour Relations in the Motor Industry*, London: George Allen and Unwin, 1967.

'Unions slow to cash in on Sex Act', *Personnel Management*, **8**, 4, April 1976, p. 13.

VAN HORN, C. W. G., 'The Hay guide chart-profile method'. *In* Rock, M. L. (Ed.), *Handbook of Wage and Salary Administration*, New York: McGraw-Hill, 1972.

VROOM, V. H. and YETTON, P. W., *Leadership and Decision-Making*, Pittsburgh: University of Pittsburgh Press, 1973.

WAINWRIGHT, D., 'Opening the door for the working woman', *Personnel Management*, **7**, 11, 16–19, 1975.

WALL, T. D. and LISCHERON, J. A., *Worker Participation*, London: McGraw-Hill, 1977.

WARMINGTON, A., 'Stress in the management of change', *In* Gowler, D. and Legge, K. (Eds.), *Managerial Stress*, Epping: Gower Press, 1975.

WASMUTH, W. J., 'Human resources administration: dilemmas of growth'. *In* Wasmuth, W. J., Simonds, R. H., Hilgert, R. L. and Lee, H. G., *Human Resource Administration: Problems of Growth and Change*, Boston: Houghton Mifflin, 1970.

WEBER, M., *The Theory of Social and Economic Organization*, translated by Parsons, T. and Henderson, A. M., New York: Free Press, 1947.

WEDDERBURN, K. W., *Company Law Reform*, (Fabian Tract 363), September 1965.

WEEKES, B., MELLISH, M., DICKENS, L. and LLOYD, J., *Industrial Relations and the Limits of Law*, Oxford: Blackwell, 1975.

WHITE PAPER, *Company Law Reform*, Cmnd. 5391, London: HMSO, July 1973.

WHITLEY, R., 'Approaches to organizational control and the "problem of order": a critique and a possible alternative', *Working Paper*, Manchester Business School, 1975.

WICKENS, J. D., 'Management by objectives: an appraisal', *Journal of Management Studies*, **5**, 365–379, 1968.

WILEMON, D. L. and GEMMILL, G. R., 'Interpersonal power in temporary management systems', *Journal of Management Studies*, **8**, 315–328, 1971.

WILSHER, P., 'The right education?', *Sunday Times, Business News*, 3 October, 1976, p. 72.

WOOD, S., 'Redundancy and stress'. *In* Gowler, D. and Legge, K. (Eds.), *Managerial Stress*, Epping: Gower Press, 1975.

WOODRUFF JR, R. L., 'Human resource accounting', *Canadian Chartered Accountant*, 156–161, September 1970.

WOODWARD, J., *Industrial Organization: Theory and Practice*, Oxford: Oxford University Press, 1965.

WOODWARD, J., *Industrial Organization: Behaviour and Control*, Oxford: Oxford University Press, 1970.

'Worrying high failure rate of sex discrimination and equal pay tribunal cases say groups', *Personnel Management*, **8**, 9, September 1976, p. 7.

YOUNGER, W. F., 'The Hay-MSL system'. *In* Bowey, A. M. (Ed.), *Handbook of Salary and Wage Systems*, Epping: Gower Press, 1975.

ZWERMAN, W. L., *New Perspectives on Organization Theory*, Westport, Conn.: Greenwood Pub. Co., 1970.

145

Subject index

Author index

Printed in Great Britain by J. W. Arrowsmith Ltd., Bristol